MORAL CRUELTY

Ameaning and the Justification of Harm

Timothy L. Hulsey
Christopher J. Frost

D1555130

University Press of America,® Inc.
Lanham · Boulder · New York · Toronto · Oxford

Library of Congress Control Number: 2004104733
ISBN 0-7618-2866-4 (paperback : alk. ppr.)

for
Aristéa

and in loving memory of
Kade

Contents

Acknowledgements

We would like to thank the many people who have helped to produce this book. Kathryn Minyard Frost and Roxanne Lee read drafts of the manuscript and offered valuable suggestions. Erin Helfert and Carmen Covington edited final drafts of the manuscript, compiled the references and contributed to the indexing of the book. Mike Arfken, Maria Czyzewska, Stan Friedman, Susan Hanson, and Yasmin Lodi made substantive contributions to particular chapters, and we have credited them accordingly on the first pages of their respective chapters. Students in two course offerings of the Texas State University Honors Program read and critiqued meaningfully early versions of the manuscript. Indeed, it is from within the crucible of the classroom that so many of the ideas contained in this work emerged with greater precision. Where we succeed in conveying a theory of moral cruelty with clarity, we have our friends, colleagues, and students to thank.

We would also like to acknowledge those who provided photographs for use in this volume. The Vietnam/Napalm photo by Nick Ut is used with permission from: AP/WIDE WORLD PHOTOS. The graphic collage, "Enron/Wall Street/Money," is used with permission from: AFSCME (special thanks to Carol Burnett, Manager of Graphics & Video). All other photographs taken by and courtesy of Christopher and Kathryn Frost.

Christopher Frost
Timothy Hulsey

Part One

Theory of
Ameaningful Morality

Chapter One

Ameaningful Morality: An Introduction

> *The hardest part in understanding the nature of evil is to first recognize*
> *that you or I could, under certain circumstances, commit many of the*
> *acts that the world has come to regard as evil. But as long as we*
> *continue to regard evildoers as a separate species, an alien category,*
> *or a wholly different type of human being, we cannot really claim to*
> *understand them.*
>
> *—R.F. Baumeister*

Although we find ourselves only three years into a new millennium, we are faced with a growing realization that much has changed in a very short time. A bipolar world dominated by nation-state superpowers has been replaced by a chaotic world adrift in a sea of terrorism, undeclared war and nameless fear. While many of the old atrocities continue to haunt us, new forms of violence and suffering seem to arise almost daily. The unrestrained avarice of Enron, Worldcom and Global Crossing, terror attacks, and the undeclared wars in Afghanistan and Iraq have led to calls for an examination of the moral structures underlying modern life (Frankl 2001; Lifton 2001).

While the atrocities we see daily on cable news channels more than justify a reexamination of 21st century morality, we suggest that this examination cannot succeed unless another, subtler phenomenon becomes part of the discourse. This phenomenon, more difficult to grasp, more difficult to perceive than overt atrocity, involves the covert cruelty practiced in ordered, "civilized" settings: actions against others that are not regarded as harmful, but seen as morally justified.

In this volume, we examine some specific mechanisms whereby humans develop moral systems that foster "justified" cruelty. Such systems may comprise all, or merely part, of an individual's overall moral system. However, in every instance, these systems relegate important moral decisions to automatic, culturally prescribed algorithms that replace individual moral reasoning with rigid application of internalized rules. Through application of such algorithms individuals may engage in harmful acts while never consciously realizing the harm they have wrought. We deem this type of moral reasoning "ameaningful."

In an ameaningful moral system, unconscious aggressive strivings and prefabricated justifications that excuse harm make crafty partners in a ceaseless dance of inflicted pain and plausible denial. The failure to perceive the unconscious dimensions of aggressive behavior serves to perpetuate socially acceptable harm. When such acts are disguised by a cloak of moral justification, *acta est fabula*. The end result is tacit approval of covertly cruel behavior masked by declarations of morally superior intent.

Such behavior, and the belief systems that underlie them, clearly deviate from the kind of intentional harm that dominates the common definition of cruelty. In fact, it is reasonable to ask whether people who commit harmful acts while failing to perceive the harm they cause are in fact evil, or merely misguided. We suggest that neither explanation is adequate and that the answer lies in a different direction. To develop this concept, we first examine the psychological bases of ameaningful morality. Here we rely heavily on the work of Sigmund Koch and his discussions of the pathology of knowledge as a basis for our understanding of the psychological dimensions of ameaningful morality. We then proceed to a consideration of the sociocultural context within which ameaningful moral systems develop. In particular, we examine the role that social systems that revere mechanical adherence to norms and rules (and that impose this reverence as a matter of course) play in perpetuating ameaningful moral reasoning systems. Third, and finally, we offer a synthesis of psychoanalytic and existential theory to explain the motivational structure of ameaningful morality.

Psychological Bases of Ameaningful Morality

In his discussions of the pathology of knowledge, Sigmund Koch offers a definition of a phenomenon he termed *ameaningful thinking* (Koch 1965; Leary 2001). It is our contention that the conditions that create ameaningful thinking mirror those that foster the development of ameaningful morality. According to Koch, *meaningful* thinking is characterized by "an organic determination of the form and substance of thought by the properties of the object and the terms of the problem. In meaningful thinking, the mind caresses, flows joyously into, over, around the relational matrix defined by the problem, the object" (Koch 1981: 79). It is important to note here Koch's emphasis on consciously mediated attention to the contextual elements of the situation as the basis for meaningful judgments about the world.

Koch fixed the locus of cognitive control squarely at the level of the individual and strongly emphasized the importance of independent thinking. In so doing, he was not advancing a disembodied, individualist point of view as some communitarian thinkers might suggest. Rather, he suggested that it is precisely the act of testing our voice against others' voices and sensibilities that connotes "independent" (i.e., meaningful) thinking (see also Polanyi 1958). To the extent that independent thought provides the only safeguard against the ideology of the collective (and against culturally prescribed cruelty), Koch postulated that meaningful thinking is not only a right, but a duty. Or, put another way, "The least evil society is that in which the general run of men are most often obliged to think while acting, have the most opportunities for exercising control over collective life as a whole, and enjoy the greatest amount of independence" (Weil 1951/1973:103).

In contrast, ameaningful thinking is dominated by mechanical processing of information, rather than mindful discovering. It is the result of a socially supplied "method" of cognition in which inquiry is so fully regulated that the rules of thinking are valued more than the thinker. "The world, or any given part of it, is not felt fully or passionately and is perceived as devoid of objective value. Ameaningful thinking relies on crutches: Rules, codes, prescriptions, rigid methods" (Koch 1981:79).

Admittedly, rules and codes, distortions and misrepresentations, are all part of the normal prejudices of cognitive categorization. As such they may represent inescapable components of cognitive functioning (DiMaggio 1997). However, ameaningful moral systems differ in that they incorporate *implicit* prejudices and exclusionary principles that escape easy detection. As Gadamer (1960/1989) expresses it, these distortions and misrepresentations reflect a "tyranny of *hidden* prejudices" (Gadamer 1960/1989: 270). It is this hidden component that lies at the core of ameaningful morality.

When based on hidden prejudices, actions may be taken before either the beliefs that produced them or their likely effects are mindfully examined. The result, when applied to moral reasoning, is a kind of moral automaticity in which genuine moral reasoning—moral reasoning guided by an authentic and contextually governed analysis of the moral elements of the situation—becomes impossible. In its place, reflexive application of internalized moral rules takes over. The product is a kind of "ameaningful morality" wherein a person reacts to potentially moral situations automatically, that is, with no conscious consideration or deliberate questioning, and thus experiences the sequence from perception to action as involuntary.

Ameaningful moral systems rely on two distinct but interrelated processes. The first is the internalization of moral rules that excuse harm against certain others under prescribed conditions. Internalization of such rules is rooted in the developmental context of childhood, generally at such an early age that meaningful processing of moral decisions is not yet possible. Such rules most often serve to allow the expression of aggressive impulses in a socially acceptable way. The second element of an ameaningful moral system is a cognitive process wherein moral situations evoke an automatic, non-conscious application of these moral codes rather than activating independent moral reasoning that considers the unique elements of the situation.

Sociocultural Bases of Ameaning

All moral systems develop within a social and historical context. Individuals gauge the appropriateness of everyday actions by the re-actions of the individuals or groups whose values they share. When behavior corresponds with acceptable social standards, considering the effects on others becomes less important, even if the actions produce harm. As we are socialized within a particular culture, biases become woven into a personal narrative—the story we tell ourselves about ourselves—that has important implications for the actions of individuals and the culture at large.

Over the course of psychological development, these habitual patterns of response come to comprise our character. Embedded within our character are nonconscious cognitive schemas, some of which provide the basis for moral decision-making. In the case of ameaningful moral systems, perception of the interpersonal world comes to be dominated by schemas containing rigid prescriptions for appropriate behavior. The result is a systematic bias in which the actions of others are automatically judged on the basis of unexamined but deeply held beliefs, rather than other plausible determinants such as cultural differences or social context.

Social conformity, clear indications that one understands and embodies the social values of the group, is inextricably woven into most personal narratives. In the context of an ameaningful moral system this means that viewing one's actions from different moral perspectives becomes unnecessary, indeed undesirable, if one's social group sanctions one's actions. Put another way, perpetrating aggression becomes acceptable as long as it is done in a socially sanctioned manner against socially sanctioned targets. In fact, if the actions are performed in a traditional manner, the harm may be conveyed covertly, out of the awareness of both the perpetrators of the harm and those who witness it. In this way, preexisting social mores provide a "moral" defense for the act. These rationales make actions ethical *of themselves.*

While the internalization of specific cultural values is a *necessary* step in the development of an ameaningful moral system, it is not a *sufficient* precondition for its development. The ability of members of a culture to engage in meaningful thought is determined, almost entirely, by the value placed by the group upon independent critical thinking. Cultures that devalue meaningful thinking explicitly and implicitly foster developmental paths that inhibit such thinking, create individuals "deprived absolutely of the possibility of achieving 'high' orders of meaningful thought, relative to their capacities, or of discriminating such states—should they occur—as in some sense valuable or even different from ameaningful thinking" (Koch 1981: 80).

Understanding how particular pieces of cultural knowledge become activated in particular situations is instructive here. Social psychologists have confirmed that cognitively–stored social constructs are accessible to the extent that they have been recently used (Hong, Morris, Chiu and Benet-Martinez 2000). Thus, frequent application of culturally supplied moral justifications becomes self-sustaining. The more a rule is applied, the more that rule gets applied.

Social systems that revere mindless adherence to norms and rules and that impose this reverence as a matter of course promote rule-bound moral reasoning. In such instances, moral inquiry may be so fully regulated that social rules displace meaningful moral reasoning about potentially moral situations. When this type of thinking becomes integrated into the character of an individual, it subordinates authentic, contextually layered moral analysis to blind application of the social rules.

For example, in American culture many messages reinforce the importance of behaving deferentially in the presence of persons higher in status or power than oneself. The covert subtext of such messages is that one may act disrespectfully to one's "inferiors" (socially defined). However, to do so is to move away from meaningful morality. As Simone Weil noted, "The supernatural virtue of justice consists of behaving exactly as though there were equality when one is the stronger in an unequal relationship" (in Frost & Bell-Metereau 1998: 13).

Cultural beliefs that eschew harm done to certain others for certain reasons may be both a cause and an effect of ameaningful moral systems. However, describing them as such does not explain *why* such systems would have value, either to individuals within a culture or to the culture as a whole. If judgments of good and evil are based on whether the actor is "like me" or "different from me," "my status" or "lower status than me," then actions (and their effects on others) are more easily ignored. As a result, the same actions performed by members of one's own social group may be judged positively, solely on the basis of group membership. The self-deception that allows individuals to ignore discrepancies in the standards applied to members and non-members may also provide a valuable tool for managing socially unacceptable thoughts and feelings.

For an example we need only revisit the acts of September 11, 2001. Those responsible for the atrocities of that day believed their actions were not only justified but holy. In framing their cause in this way, they gave voice to a belief system in which "others," in this case non-Muslims, were suitable to be punished precisely because of their otherness. The oppression and violence that sometimes arises from U.S. foreign policy in the Middle East was cited as the essential provocation for these acts. The violent response to this perceived evil was judged righteous *because of its source*, rather than its nature. The perverse element here is that many of the responses to the bombing of the Pentagon and World Trade Center were of similar, if not identical structure. To respond by bombing one country (Afghanistan), and then launching a "preemptive strike" against another (Iraq, a country having only the most tenuous of connections to the bombing), are likewise adjudged righteous because of their source.

Those who perpetrated the attacks saw themselves as absolutely virtuous and those they attacked as absolutely evil. Those currently retaliating see themselves as absolutely virtuous and those they are attacking as absolutely evil. Both groups believe themselves justified in their actions because of the perceived righteousness conveyed by their moral belief system. In this way they each ignore the fact that retaliation makes them guilty of precisely the behaviors they claim to despise. At the same time, they are able to embody the aggressive strivings of a particular cultural group, forbidden by the same code of moral beliefs from acting aggressively in other circumstances, against other individuals.

The cultural rules that allow aggression against certain others begin from a familiar starting point: Humans almost unerringly locate sources of evil in others. Evil exists in other people, other races, and other religions (Dasgupta & Greenwald 2001; Devine 1989; Lott 2002; Pettigrew & Meertens 1995; Tajfel 1982). By contrast, the notion of good is typically embedded in the self and its cultural and interpersonal identifications. "My family," "My country," "My religion," are commonly voiced allegiances. However, the price for these allegiances often includes group tolerance of aggression against different others; indeed, such aggressive acts may foster group solidarity. And by engaging in such acts "automatically" we may be virtually unaware of the damage done.

Existential Anxiety and Ameaningful Morality

As Freud (1960) argued, humans are psychologically obliged to find ways to express disturbing impulses. Deriving as they do from urges deemed unacceptable by one's social group, however, such impulses cannot be conveyed directly. To retain status within one's social group requires adherence to the shared rules. Expressions of unacceptable impulses such as aggression or lust can occur only indirectly, only within the bound of socially acceptable behavior, and, preferably, in a manner that obscures the original motive. Freud describes how the use of parapraxes (unconsciously motivated actions) gives voice to aggressive impulses.

> In healthy people, egoistic, jealous and hostile feelings
> and impulses, on which the pressure of moral education
> weighs heavily, make frequent use of the pathway provided by
> parapraxes in order to find some expression for their strength,
> which undeniably exists, but is not recognized by the higher
> mental agencies. Acquiescence in these parapraxes and
> chance actions is to a large extent equivalent to a compliant
> tolerance of the immoral (Freud 1960: 276).

Since most moral systems explicitly reject the direct expression of aggression, other, less obvious mechanisms must be employed. By allowing ourselves to use, albeit unconsciously, seemingly unintentional actions to express these impulses we are, Freud argued, allowing ourselves an outlet to behave in "immoral" ways. Since we experience the action as unintentional, we are perfectly positioned to deny responsibility for any attendant harm the action may "unintentionally" produce.

Terror management theory, a more recent theoretical synthesis of psychoanalysis, existentialism, evolutionary psychology, and cognitive dissonance theory (Festinger 1957), explores the roots of this phenomenon even further. The fundamental assumption of terror management theory is that human cognitive complexity creates the conditions necessary for freedom of reactivity (Arndt, Goldenberg, Greenberg, Pyszcynski, & Solomon 2000). Humans are, by virtue of these highly evolved cognitive capacities, able to separate responses from the stimuli that initiate them, and thereby, choose from a variety of possible reactions. The ability to imagine future events, to pursue dreams, and to regulate thoughts, feelings, and actions through abstract and symbolic thought grants humans the remarkable powers required to negotiate the demands of a complex social environment. It also enables us to initiate actions that follow from voluntary decisions, from meaningful reasoning.

Self awareness and cognitive complexity, however, exact a price. Because as humans we consciously experience our own existence, we must also acknowledge our mortality. As Becker (1973) observed, the awareness of the certainty of death creates a special, uniquely human anxiety—the existential dilemma. And the dilemma underscores the angst of freedom itself: On what basis do I choose? What shall be the outcome of my choice? What if I choose badly?

Humans respond to this dilemma by creating shared worldviews (*Weltanschauung*) as shields against existential dread. Such worldviews are "humanly created beliefs about the nature of reality shared by groups of people that are developed as a means by which the people manage the potential for terror (hence our term terror management) engendered by the human awareness of mortality" (Arndt et al. 2000: 206). Because such shared worldviews provide a reassuring armor against death anxiety, they become sacred icons of both personal and social psychology. Identification with the worldview comes to be perceived as a singular measure of personal worth within a culture. Self-esteem is tied to the ability to successfully embody and defend the values of the culture. Thus, adherence to cultural standards translates directly to both self worth and social status.

The social becomes the psychological when individuals internalize the values and goals of the culture. Members of a social group defend shared ideals with the same rage and aggression with which they defend life itself. A shared sense of belief, and of the sacred, creates a sense of shared power. Individuals aspire, by virtue of beliefs shared with important others, to embody the strength of the whole group. As Erich Fromm (1973) noted, shared cultural beliefs become objects of devotion, our sacred icons. If shared beliefs are to protect against death awareness, they must be protected against all threats–particularly those represented by divergent beliefs. Thus, groups (and the individuals who comprise the groups) are strongly motivated to maintain these beliefs and defend them against threats. Indeed, the greater the threat to self-esteem, the more powerfully individuals will seek to identify with their social group. And, conversely, as ingroup biases increase, the better group members feel about themselves (Fein, Hoshino-Brown, Davies & Spencer 2003). Returning to Arndt et al. (2000):

> From this perspective, human beings' lurid and longstanding
> traditions of hostility and disdain toward anyone different than
> themselves can best be understood as egregious manifestations
> of the defenses marshaled against the threats different others
> pose to the self-esteem-producing, anxiety-reducing, death-
> denying properties of one's cultural worldview (2000: 210).

As we noted before, members of a group respond to threats to their worldview as an attack against the sacred and, thus, as an attack against life itself.

Death awareness creates two levels of psychological concern. The first is a literal awareness of our own mortality. The second is metaphysical, underscoring the angst created by choice and individual freedom. The latter relates to ameaningful moral systems directly. Each time an individual chooses, he or she simultaneously "loses" all alternatives that were not chosen. Every other alternative becomes effectively "dead."

Sharing beliefs with important others facilitates the repression of death awareness by operating as a covert defense against existential anxiety. Because they operate outside conscious awareness, these beliefs may be activated without initiating conscious moral reasoning. To face death awareness (literal or metaphysical) consciously requires perceiving and engaging the pursuant anxiety. But avoiding existential anxiety in this way comes at a cost: Independent reasoning (making complex individual decisions within a social crucible) is discouraged in favor of blind application of the anxiety-ridding social rules.

In his *Science of Logic*, Hegel (1976) argues for a connection between death and individuality: "The nature of finite things as such is to have the seed of their passing away as their essential being: the hour of their birth is the hour of their death" (Hegel 1976: 142). This idea receives further confirmation in Freud's writings:

> Freud's theory of anxiety brings birth and death together as separation crises. Freud is thus moving toward a structural analysis of organic life as being constituted by a dialectic between unification and separation or interdependence. The principle of unification or interdependence sustains the immortal life of the species and the mortal life of the individual; the principle of separation or independence gives the individual his individuality and ensures his death.
>
> If death gives life individuality and if man is the organism that represses death, then man is the organism that represses his own individuality (Brown 1959/1985: 105).

Brown (1959/1985) goes on to argue that human social organizations exist primarily to "save" individuals from the burden of individual choice, an "escape from freedom" in Erich Fromm's language (Fromm 1941). He sees the creation of social groups as an inherently repressive act, fostering as it does a flight from death and the fear of separation and individuality and offering in its stead a kind of group immortality (and by extension, individual immortality) via a shared history and a common religion. Under conditions of communal repression, the death instinct must operate underground, malignantly. If death is what gives life its individuality, then the repression of death awareness creates a flight away from independence and separateness, and at the same time prompts "the compulsive return of the repressed [aggressive] impulse" (Brown 1959/1985: 109).

As with all impulses, aggression seeks expression. Contained, however, within the strictures of social rules, aggression will only be tolerated within specified parameters, against certain targets, under certain conditions. It is this permissible aggression that provides the basis for moral cruelty, and that constitutes the principle result of ameaningful morality. Social structures that unduly bind existential anxiety do so at the cost of repressing aggression (and, by extension, individuality). Repressed aggression seeks expression and, as a symptomatic compromise, cultural rules allow cruelty against some, typically outsiders, without sanction. The more closely the rules are followed when expressing aggression, the greater the cultural forgiveness for the act. And, as Freud (1960) noted, individuals (and societies) become ill when they seek to evade anxiety through unconscious mechanisms.

So where does this leave us? St. Benedict urged, "Keep death daily before your eyes" (in Norris 2001). Managing the anxiety created by the existential dilemma requires a kind of bi-directional gaze. This gaze must at once consider both the goals of the individual and the goals of the social group to which the individual belongs. It must also concurrently evaluate the effects of these goals on the accuracy of self- and other-perception. We must develop an ability to see both ourselves and our intentions without losing sight of others or the likely effects of our actions on them.

To develop a bi-directional gaze is to hone the ability to distinguish figure from ground, to recognize our intentions as we direct attention to others. As difficult as this may be, to speak of complexity and elusiveness is not to speak of impossibility. Individuals are born into a social crucible. If we examine how parents interact with children in ways that promote meaningful moral reasoning, if we discover educational methods that promote meaningful engagement, if we identify religious training that promotes active and meaningful moral reasoning, if we demand media coverage of "patriotism" and "national pride" more conducive to meaningful civic engagement than mindless obedience to political agendas, we will shift the focus toward meaningful moral engagement.

While there may be no final litmus test to distinguish meaning from ameaning, the continuing levels of moral cruelty—harm done in the name of the good—suggests that the task is an urgent one. Having laid out the basic structure of ameaningful moral reasoning, we now turn to a more detailed analysis of its consequences, morally cruel acts. Then, in Part II of this volume, we address the task of fleshing out the skeleton of ameaningful reasoning that begins in infancy and culminates in social institutional reality.

Chapter Two

Moral Cruelty

If it were so simple! If only there were evil people somewhere insidiously committing evil deeds, and it were necessary only to separate them from the rest of us and destroy them. But the line separating good and evil runs through the heart of every human being. And who is willing to destroy a piece of his own heart?

—*Alexander Solzhenitsyn*

We use moral systems to guide our thoughts and behaviors. Our moral beliefs define which actions are moral. However, when our moral code allows us to harm others without suffering social sanction, a kind of "moral cruelty" may ensue. Moral cruelty involves actions that are sanctioned by the individual's culture, but which, from most other perspectives, would be seen as cruel. Such codes allow the expression of aggressive impulses in socially acceptable ways.

The concept of moral cruelty also suggests that in many "normal" patterns of interaction there exists a necessary and crucial, but hidden and implicit, element of sadism. Not sexual sadism, but a kind of moral sadism wherein expression of aggressive impulses that are forbidden in most situations may be gratified under certain, culturally prescribed circumstances.

Morality is intertwined with awareness. When conscious awareness and perceptual tendencies become directed toward the culturally-prescribed interpretation of an event, individual moral sensitivity may be reduced. In such instances, the contextual elements of the situation that would, under normal circumstances, help render its meaning are subsumed by a focus on prepackaged rationales. Rather than wrestling with the moral implications of certain actions and bridging the gap between abstract moral principles and concrete life events, individuals can instead attend simply to the moral justifications that validate their actions. Moral cruelty develops as individuals learn to focus on the *rationales* for behaviors rather than the *effects*.

Consider the case of the Reverend John Plummer. Many years before entering the ministry, Lieutenant Plummer was a proud and successful U.S. Army helicopter pilot and operations officer serving in Vietnam. His image of himself at the time was that of a dutiful soldier, fighting under the flag of his country and defending the values for which it stood. On June 8, 1972, Plummer ordered a routine airstrike on Trang Bang, Vietnam, a village about twenty-five miles west of Saigon. After the strike, which included both explosives and napalm, Plummer reported satisfaction with the results. He had dutifully executed his role as an officer, allowing him to look toward the next bombing campaign, to direct his attention elsewhere.

The morning after the airstrike, however, a photograph appeared on the front page of the military newspaper, *Stars and Stripes*. Taken by photographer Nick Ut and destined to win a Pulitzer Prize, the picture showed terrified children fleeing the village of Trang Bang. The central figure in the photograph, a young and terrified Pham Thi Kim Phuc, runs naked, her clothes burned away by napalm. Her eyes are closed, blinded, while her mouth is torn open by screams of terror and pain.

Not surprisingly, many soldiers, politicians, and citizens were unmoved by the photograph. After all, although war is hell, the cause is just. When Plummer saw the picture, however, it knocked him to his knees. His image of himself as a proud soldier performing his duty was shattered by the unremitting reality of that photograph.

The litany of patriotic phrases rolled out for such occasions failed to mask the anguish in the face of one little girl. Instead, the inherent cruelty of the act became obvious. Ut's compelling image triggered a perceptual shift: Plummer was suddenly faced with the harm his dutiful actions had created. The moral rationale no longer automatically excused the harm he had done. Plummer was forced to construct a new moral narrative, this time one *of his own making.*

In instances such as these it is important to remember that ameaningful morality is not amorality. Lieutenant Plummer was, by all conventional measures, a moral man. Rather, his actions suggest allegiance to a "*destructive moral structure*" (Lifton 2001), one that separates actions from their effects and excuses harmful actions performed for culturally sanctioned reasons. It is this separation between moral abstraction and concrete life events that creates the possibility for moral cruelty. Of course, activation of non-conscious ameaningful moral algorithms does not necessarily lead to moral cruelty. When such algorithms contain within them a prescription for harm, however, morally cruel acts are likely to result.

The creation and internalization of shared social codes is an important part of the development of societies and individuals. However, there often appears to be a toxic element in "normal" patterns of socialization that values and promotes ameaningful moral reasoning and, as a result, a disjunction between belief and action. In such instances habitual patterns of harm may parade under a banner of social normalcy. Within the parameters of socially acceptable cruelty, individuals may actively and intentionally seek to control, suppress, punish, and hurt others, but camouflage the harm behind a veil of culturally supplied moral justification. As Ross observes in *The Sadomasochism of Everyday Life* (1997):

> What is most civil and cultivated in people can easily enough degenerate into moral sadism and a scorn for impurity. Moral rectitude can give rise to prejudice, oppression, xenophobia . . . unnecessary violence, demoralization, self-loathing and indiscriminate destruction . . . (1997: 153).

Externalizing Evil

It is within the context of acculturation and shared beliefs that ameaningful moral systems are created. Just as acculturation may produce valued (and valuable) propensities for altruism or generosity, it may also foment bigotry and hatred. What distinguishes moral cruelty from generic cruelty is the cloak of moral decency lent to the act by cultural rules that excuse certain types of harm against certain types of people.

Ameaningful moral codes frequently categorize "other-ness" not merely as undesirable, but as evil: ([1]**evil:** *adjective, a: The antithesis of GOOD in all its principal senses. In OE., as in all the other early Teut. langs. exc. Scandinavian, this word is the most comprehensive adjectival expression of disapproval, dislike, or disparagement. (OED, 2ed.).* Ameaningful moral systems often reserve the most severe forms of "disapproval, dislike, and disparagement" for those outside one's social group. Considerable evidence illustrates this point, documenting how humans exclude, devalue, and discount those designated as "other" (Lott 2002). As Eliot Aronson puts it:

Despite their best efforts to be open-minded, many otherwise decent people are still capable of subtle acts of prejudice. Indeed, many investigators believe that indirect–and perhaps more insidious–forms of prejudice have largely replaced the blatant kinds of racial bigotry expressed by many white Americans in the past. Today, most people probably think of themselves as unprejudiced, even though they may continue to discriminate in less obvious ways (1999: 322).

Or, to quote Jonathon Glover's "Humanity: A Moral History of the 20th. Century:"

[Human] moralities are 'internal', giving weight to the interests of those inside a community, but doing little against the common indifference or even hostility towards those outside. . . . It is increasingly obvious that this moral gap is a human disaster (Glover 2000: 28).

Recent research into motivated social perception bears this out. In a series of studies, Fein and his colleagues (2003) found that threats to self image provoke specific and predictable changes in social perception. In particular, they found that participants whose self-esteem was threatened attempted to maintain their self image by applying stereotyped thinking to others in their social environment (Fein et al. 2003).

The activation of stereotyped social perception in reaction to threats to self-esteem acted to buffer the participants' feelings of lowered self worth by increasing their sense of belonging to an in-group. The resulting activation of a negative stereotype then led the participants to derogate individuals not perceived to be members of their group. The activation of these implicit belief structures allowed participants to "see the target through biased eyes without consciously realizing they were doing it. Thus, in a sense, they could have their cake (applying a negative stereotype) and eat it too (avoiding guilt or recrimination)" (Fein et al. 2003: 29).

In considering the social and political events that followed the September 11th attack, we find that some Americans responded automatically with prescribed moral codes like "an eye for an eye." The result was predictable: Millions of people whose religious beliefs speak of loving one's enemies, praying for those who persecute, and turning the other cheek, began praying for divine blessing on a retaliatory military campaign. Attending to an ancient moral code that justified base impulses (vengeance and violence) created a moral camouflage that justified a military response while obfuscating the deeper moral dilemmas that such a response created.

Others, however, began to grasp for a different framework within which to understand the events of that day. Searching for meaning in a seemingly meaningless act, many embraced active moral reasoning in a new and active way. They watched the news more closely than ever before, scoured websites on central Asia and Islam, and wondered what could have possibly motivated such hatred and violence. Suddenly, paying attention to the world beyond national borders and to moral responsibility in the face of evil became necessary. As old habits of attention were cast away, new concerns about death, as well as questions about what constitutes a meaningful life, emerged.

Why did this transformation in social and moral awareness occur? The empirical literature on moral awareness is only marginally helpful here. Focusing on the interpretive systems used to determine whether a given situation includes moral dimensions, Thoma and colleagues (1991) found that reasoning about justice, social convention, care issues, and religious prescription lies at the heart of moral awareness. In examining these interpretive systems, the authors set out to determine which systems inform the action phase of moral behavior and the ways individuals solve moral dilemmas. Rather than focusing on how interpretive systems shape awareness of the moral dimensions of a situation, they focused on those components that affect the *responses* to the moral dimensions of life.

As interpretive systems, moral codes alert us to various aspects of the moral world. However, relying as they do on preexisting moral schemata, activation of these systems may still limit the ability to see the unique moral dimensions of a situation. Individuals may perceive the event in terms of prevailing, culturally sanctioned biases. In such cases, individual moral reasoning, based on concrete actualities of the situation, continues to be elusive.

Perceiving Moral Cruelty

To reverse Arrendt's chilling phrase, to look under the covers of moral cruelty means to focus on the evil of banality—the toxic elements hidden within the fabric of everyday life. Doing so requires an ability to change perceptual lenses or, to borrow the language of social-cognitive psychology, a way to induce *frame switching*: to become aware that a situation possesses a moral dimension that will then activate independent moral reasoning. Persons who react to moral dilemmas on the basis of careful moral reasoning, and are aware that they are doing so, differ from persons who react automatically to moral situations on the basis of non-conscious devotion to an ameaningful moral code.

Activating independent moral reasoning is not a straightforward endeavor, however. Emotional experience and moral reasoning are tied together so intimately that they appear to possess shared neural pathways in the brain (Helmuth 2001). Since the emotional reality of a situation must be recognized before moral reasoning is activated, individuals must first perceive the emotional essence of an event in order to pierce the self-deception that precedes morally justified cruelty. The problem, however, is this: Humans search their environment for information that confirms preexisting beliefs, both about the world and themselves. This perceptual tendency is even more pronounced when facing threats to the self-concept.

> Social judgments serve *symbolic functions*, in that those judgments carry a number of implicit messages about the person making the judgment. Thus, when people assess whether other individuals are smart or dumb, moral or immoral, capable or incompetent, they are wary about what those assessments say about their own character and ability. Thus, they 'manage' their judgments of others to reach conclusions that symbolically maintain or bolster images, usually positive ones, that they possess about their own competence and character. In a phrase, people often work to make sure that their evaluations of other people are implicit acts of self-affirmation (in the same sense that Steele 1988, refers to). To be sure, people do form social judgments to

make their social worlds predictable and controllable,
but those social judgments must navigate around certain
'sacred beliefs' that people possess about themselves.
One's judgments must either affirm those beliefs, or at the least not
contradict them (Dunning 2003: 47).

Individuals first look within themselves for definitions of
"successful" or "moral" and then project those attributes onto those
whom their culture admires, finding in their icons images of themselves
(Dunning 2003). If all goes well, this kind of deception allows us (and
others) to believe that we are exactly the kind of people our culture most
values, while, in many cases, fostering a social and personal agenda that
values discreet self-promotion above all. As Glover observes, "People
benefit from seeming, rather than from being, moral" (2000: 20).

Individuals facilitate their own self-deception by adhering to
belief systems that support preexisting biases. These belief systems are
internalized through developmental socialization experiences, becoming
part of the perceptual mechanism. Once internalized, these systems are
engaged automatically, bypassing individual reasoning. The result is
the automatic application of social rules that provides both the cover to
act in morally cruel ways and the mechanism whereby awareness of the
aggressive component of the behavior may be suppressed.

Assembling the covert pieces of the dialogical puzzle means
first examining the social and moral context of events. The same event,
viewed from two differing perspectives, may produce diametrically
opposed conclusions.

Consider . . . two boys rapidly contracting the eyelids of
their right eyes. In one, this is an involuntary twitch; in the
other a conspiratorial signal to a friend. The two movements
are, as movements, identical. Yet the difference, however
unphotographable, between a twitch and a wink is vast; as
anyone unfortunate enough to have had the first taken for the
second knows.
That, however, is just the beginning. Suppose. . . there
is a third boy [who parodies the first two by contracting his
eyelids, and then practices doing so at home as well]; this

boy is neither winking nor twitching, [but] parodying. . . and rehearsing. . . . Complexities are possible, if not practically without end, at least logically so (Geertz 1973: 6-7).

Examining moral acts in context brings us to the perceptual core of moral cruelty—a vantage from which we can distinguish a twitch from a wink. Moral cruelty occurs within a context: conditions evoke a non-conscious, moral coda that in turn produces a harmful behavioral response and, *at the same time*, prevents the individual from realizing the harm inherent in the act. Changing the vantage so that the individual may perceive both the event (the cruel act) and the context for that event (the automatic, non-conscious response) renders the aggression inherent in such acts immediately apparent. The viewer becomes aware of both the nature of the act and the unthinking manner in which he or she responded. This changed perspective creates the possibility of independent moral reasoning outside the ameaningful moral system.

So what is it precisely that *limits* the ability to switch frames, to attend to multiple dimensions (and multiple meanings) of any given perceptual display? There appear to be at least two immediate factors at play: sensory adaptation and selective moral attention. Sensory adaptation refers to the tendency to cease attending to unchanging or constant sources of stimulation and, instead, direct attention to new or novel stimuli. When humans are exposed repeatedly to violence, desensitization to the violence often results. The more that violence pervades the perceptual field (whether real or fictionalized), the more muted the emotional response (Cline et. al. 1973; Thomas 1982; Thomas, Lippicott & Drabman 1977).

Eliot Aronson (1976) beautifully and honestly illustrated the link between desensitization (sensory adaptation) and ameaningful morality in his classic text, *The Social Animal*:

> [While watching the news about the use of napalm on a Vietnamese village], my oldest son, who was about 10 at the time, asked brightly, "Hey, Dad, what's napalm?"
>
> "Oh," I answered casually, "as I understand it, it's a chemical that burns people; it also sticks so that if it gets on your skin, you can't remove it." And I continued to watch the news.

> A few minutes later, I happened to glance at my son and
> saw tears streaming down his face. Struck by my son's pain
> and grief, I grew dismayed as I began to wonder what had
> happened to me. Had I become so brutalized that I could
> answer my son's question so matter-of-factly—as if he had
> asked me how a baseball is made or how a leaf functions?
> Had I become so accustomed to human brutality that I could
> be casual in its presence (1976: 253-254)?

The news program Aronson was watching might well have been a
recounting of Trang Bang. Whereas Plummer was "knocked to his knees"
by a photograph, Aronson's sensory adaptation to violence was shaken
by the tears of a child.

In discussing sensory adaptation, cognitive psychologists point
toward an evolutionary basis, a kind of survival value if you will. Humans
adapt, or habituate, by ignoring unchanging stimuli that pose no peril in
order to perceive better new information that might signal a threat. In
like manner, the presence of selectively attentive cognition is also said
to possess survival value. Because the brain cannot attend to all stimuli
present at any given moment, it screens out the "noise" in favor of the
"signal."

Applying this process to moral attention provides the necessary
perceptual foundation for the mindless application of social rules that
underpins morally cruel behavior. *Moral reasoning tasks are turned over
to automatic cognitive processes created through social learning and
shaped by avaricious unconscious drives.* These automatic processes
activate the non-conscious application of ameaningful moral rules that
allows for gratification of the impulses in a manner that maintains or
enhances social standing.

William James understood this process well. In referring to
those stimuli to which individuals attend at the expense of competing
information that they ignore, James (1890/1950) reasoned that if a thing
presented to a person a thousand times goes completely unnoticed by the
individual, it cannot be said to enter his experience. A person's "empirical
thought depends on the things he has experienced, but what these shall be
is to a large extent determined by his habits of attention" (p. 286). James

concluded that all of consciousness—the sense of meaning, the very sense of self—must be constructed from the stimuli to which individuals have attended. The *meaning* derived from the experience of life, the *consciousness* that is the stream of this ongoing experience, and the *self* that is constructed as a personal representation of that consciousness all depend upon habits of attention.

Extending James, habits of attention may also be connected to habits of moral awareness. As Simone Weil noted, "the massacre of one hundred thousand Chinese hardly alters the order of the world as they perceive it, but if instead a fellow worker has a slight rise in pay which they have not, the order of the world is turned upside down! . . . What is generally named egoism is not love of self, it is a defect of perspective" (1957: 133). By attending to moral principles in the abstract, yet acting habitually in accordance with "normal" social rules, a person can easily and seamlessly cause harm, yet never perceive the harm because his attention was focused on the abstraction. By refining the understanding of this behavior vis-a-vis moral cruelty, we may extend our definition of morality: *Morality begins at the moment of perception. What individuals choose to attend to, or fail to attend to, of itself constitutes a moral dimension in life.*

Likewise, building upward from simple acts of attention to broader patterns of perception extends the concept of character: *Character refers not only to coherent patterns of action, but to coherent patterns of perceiving as well.* Just as a given act of attention presupposes a moral choice, so a meaningful moral system inevitably entails a keen moral sensibility.

In distinguishing between meaningful and ameaningful thinking, Koch (1981) cautioned that algorithms designed to assess reasoning as meaningful or ameaningful cannot be constructed in advance; knowing is sensibility–dependent. Accordingly, a "moral codes" perspective on learned morality represents an algorithmic attempt to specify in advance what is moral. Algorithmic moral schemas may create and perpetuate an inability to see actions within the context of broader concerns. The moral code is perceived as the figure, but the background has been lost.

A person committed to meaningful thought and meaningful moral reasoning must necessarily struggle with the gap between abstract principles and the particular, concrete events of life. Because this infinite variety of life events cannot, even in principle, be specified in advance, a simple correspondence between a formalized rule and a concrete event can never exist. Indeed, Koch argued that this is true even in the scientific pursuit of knowledge about the physical world:

> What results from this single-minded pursuit of [rule-bound, rational reconstruction] is a view which progressively attenuates the human inquirer into an abstraction–ultimately a coincidental one, whose presence can seem a mere unhygienic complication (Koch 1999: 8-9).

The infinite range of possible life events, each of which may be perceived from a multitude of perspectives, underscores the enormity of the perceptual task. As a result, formalized moral coda seldom if ever accurately address a specific moment of experience. Rather, meaningful moral decisions rely on conscious awareness of the moral dimensions of a situation as lived and the activation of independent moral reasoning about the specific situation and the context within which it occurs. Systems of moral thought do not bridge the gap between morality and action; people do.

Thus, the concept of moral attention involves elements of both volition and learning. The innermost core of moral cruelty hinges on a specific aspect of perception: Under what conditions are persons most able to switch perceptual frames, to learn to attend to a different subset of information in order to perceive the moral dimensions of a situation more accurately? And how and when does this frame switching occur in situations where people suddenly perceive what they do not want to see? Whether we are talking about the bombing of a Vietnamese village, flying an airliner full of innocent people into the World Trade Centers (or a violent reaction to the same), or simply relating to those around us, the challenge of moral attention confronts us constantly.

Part Two

Ameaning
in Life Context

Chapter Three

Childrearing: Developmental Roots of Ameaning

My family is a microcosm of the culture. What is writ large in the destruction of the biosphere was writ small in the destruction of our household. This is one way the destructiveness propagates itself—the sins of the fathers (and mothers) visiting themselves unto the children for seven generations, or seven times seven generations. The death of my childhood may have been dramatic, but in a nation in which 565,000 children are killed or injured by their parents or guardians each year, my childhood does not qualify as remarkably abnormal. Another way to say this is that within any culture that destroys the salmon, that commits genocide, that demands wage slavery, most of the individuals—myself included—are probably to a greater or lesser degree insane.

—Derrick Jensen

Picture the scene: An elderly man and his donkey slowly making their way toward a small Moroccan village. Following a well-worn trail, no more than a narrow rut really, they both know the way. Still the man perceives a need to keep the animal on track. Gripping a well-worn board, about one-inch by one-inch square and five feet long, he swings without thinking. If the donkey leans to the left, he smacks the left buttock. If the donkey strays to the right, a blow to the right buttock is equally certain. And, should the donkey slow its pace, a corrective blow is delivered to the rear.

Like our man with the donkey, when parents understand parenting primarily in terms of watching over the creature in their charge, directing it down the straight and narrow path, and correcting any movement out of the well-established rut of tradition, they participate materially in perpetuating the moral automaticity that defines ameaningful morality. This process is a dialectical one. Parents knowingly and unknowingly bring their own moral sensibility to bear on childrearing. Their approach in turn shapes the child's understanding of what is moral, transmitting a parenting narrative to the next generation.

This is not to suggest that parents intentionally inculcate reprehensible moral rules into their parenting styles. Rather, parents were once children too. As such, they incorporated the implicit and explicit moral narratives of their families into their own ways of thinking about and behaving in the world. When these moral systems contain prescriptions for acceptable harm and a requirement that beliefs be unquestioningly accepted, the seeds of "toxic parenting" are planted. When these ideas become part of the grown child's own parenting style, they are transmitted to yet another generation of future parents.

Ameaningful moral systems become instilled in children when over-controlling (authoritarian) parents inculcate rigid moral values and do so in a way that clearly communicates that such values must be accepted, internalized, and, above all, never questioned. These are the two necessary steps in the equation: internalizing directly an intolerant moral system and learning that it must not be questioned (which, in turn, facilitates the moral automaticity that fosters ameaningful moral reasoning). The seeds of ameaningful morality are planted when childrearing practices encourage the unquestioning acceptance of moral decision-making rules. The creation of a system dominated by mindless application of these rules begins when obedience supplants engagement as the basis for the child's developing sense of morality. When obedience becomes the singular measure of "good" behavior, the child internalizes a moral narrative characterized by rigid applications of learned rules, rather than by contextually bound appraisals of potentially moral situations. The ability to employ moral reasoning appropriate to a specific context is quashed, replaced by automatic responses reflexively activated by the narrative.

Careful definition of ameaningful moral systems and the moral cruelty they may create is an essential step in discussing the broader social and psychological effects of these systems. However, identifying the root causes of such systems represents an even more important challenge. If ameaningful moral systems exist, then they must have an identifiable developmental pathway, a pathway that can be discovered and described. In so doing, the critical role of the family–the crucible of individual development–becomes a logical point of departure.

> Since authoritarian society reproduces itself in the individual structures of the masses with the help of the authoritarian family, it follows that political reaction has to regard and defend the authoritarian family as the basis of the 'state culture, and civilization...' [It is] political reaction's germ cell, the most important centre for the production of reactionary men and women. Originating and developing from definite social processes, it becomes the most essential institution for the preservation of the authoritarian system that shapes it (Reich 1941: 104-105).

Evolutionary explanations of human behavior notwithstanding, the fundamental role of early socialization experiences in shaping individual attitudes, beliefs and character is not subject to serious debate (Harton & Bourgeois 2004; Lau, Lee & Chiu 2004). The role of parenting in creating the psychological self is critical. Parents shape experience directly through behavioral modification and social learning. They also facilitate the internalization of important emotional and interpersonal styles by modeling interactional styles (children observe how their parents relate to them and to others) and by interacting in particular ways with the children themselves. Ethical and moral beliefs likewise emerge within the crucible of the family. Parents inform children about acceptable behavior directly and model moral decision-making for their children. Children, in turn, are affected by what they are told is moral, what behaviors are reinforced (or punished), and the moral behavior they see practiced by their parents.

Ameaningful Parenting

To uncover the developmental roots of ameaningful moral systems, we must look within the family system to discern the ways in which the development of moral systems is affected by parenting. Numerous authors have investigated the parenting styles that foster what we have identified as ameaningful moral reasoning (cf. Ariés 1962; de Mause 1974; Schatzman 1973; Helfer and Kempe 1980; and Moustakas 1972). What these authors offer is a clear perception of the often harmful subtext of "normal" childrearing practices.

> Sometime ago I became interested in the study of alienation and loneliness especially among children in schools and hospitals. . . . I saw the spontaneous expressions of young children change into apathy and reserve, the vigorous, spirited involvement in learning and living change into mechanical, deathlike behavior. I saw grown-ups reward and punish, sometimes with the direct use of authority and sometimes with subtle and devious methods. I saw a child's right to express his own identity and to grow as a unique person throttled by loud, demanding orders and by sweet, manipulating words.
>
> What shocked me then and shocks me still is that in spite of all the evidence that alienation poisons, reduces, and limits the self, authoritarian people continue to impose their standards and values on others; they think they should direct and control what a child learns and how he learns. Not only do. . . these parents. . . shrewdly and efficiently manage to restrain and deny freedom of choice, but they actually kill sources of life, which when unfettered and free enhance the individuality, uniqueness, and integrity of the self. The official spokesmen of our society still delude themselves with the belief that the docile submission to rules and external standards is still the best basis for human relations and for responsible living. They believe this in spite of the destruction and unhappiness that surround them . . . (Moustakas 1972: 26-27).

Three specific assumptions about the parent-child relationship are implicit in this model of parenting: 1) a "master-slave" model for the parent-child relationship, reflected by the power distance between parent and child; 2) an equating of obedience with goodness; and 3) a belief that the means of parenting—including ones that produce anxiety, shame, insecurity, or helplessness in the child—are justified by the end (i.e., socially acceptable behavior).

Assumption 1: Power is the most effective basis for the parent-child relationship. Parental power provides the motivational leverage for parents and may be used to coerce children's conformity. Perhaps the most tangible manifestation of this assumption is the continuing use of corporal punishment. In the 1990s, a survey of parents in the United States revealed that 84% of the respondents believed that a good spanking every few months is needed to raise obedient children (Straus & Donnelly 1994). Note the almost unprecedented level of agreement here (approaching unanimity) in a country that is fractiously divided on virtually all value issues. Moreover, spanking continues to be widely practiced despite the overwhelming evidence of its harmful consequences (Gershoff 2002).

When questioned why they spank, most respondents in Straus's periodic surveys said that they spank as a means of communicating which actions are acceptable and which actions are not. They used spanking to communicate to the child that actions have consequences. When a child touches something hot, for example, the burn itself is the consequence. The child learns not to touch things that are hot. Where consequences are not evident (breaking a parent's valued object), or where consequences are severe (running into a street), parents must themselves supply the consequences necessary for learning.

Assumption 2: Obedience and conformity are extremely valuable—so valuable that they must be inculcated against the child's will. In many families obedience and "goodness" are synonymous. Underneath this assumption lies a critically important, but often unexamined assumption: There exists only one way of being in the world, a straight and narrow path along which a child must be directed. According to a vast literature produced by 20th century scholars, the opposite of this assumption is closer to the truth. There are a variety of ways of being in the world. Children differ along many personality dimensions, including introversion and extraversion, thinking and feeling, sensing and intuiting, openness to experience and need for structure. These differences point to the need to embrace an open-ended process of individuation—a facilitation of the natural unfolding of character—not to a need for standardization and homogenization. By perceiving childhood as a multitude of potential paths, one recognizes that establishing a parenting structure appropriate to the temperament of the child allows us to relate to the child dialogically. As the child interrelates with parents and with others, exploring the reality of self and world, she constructs her own sense of self within a system that respects and safeguards her well-being.

Returning to the image of the donkey, we see that it is not just the board that comprises the cruelty. Rather, the cruelty begins with the perception of a path, a rut, into which all individuals must be channeled. To treat everyone the same, when people are in fact different, is one of the core components of ameaningful moral narratives. Once individual differences are perceived, this familiar injunction against cruelty—against sadism—requires a refinement: "Treat everyone as they wish to be treated."

To the extent that we succeed, the outcome will parallel the one Alice Miller wishes for her readers:

> [Readers] will locate the places where the seeds of cruelty have been sown and by virtue of their discovery will conclude that the human race need not remain the victim of such cruelty forever. For, by uncovering the unconscious rules of the power game and the methods by which it attains legitimacy, we are certainly in a position to bring about basic changes (1983: 62).

Assumption 3: The means of parenting—including ones that produce anxiety, shame, insecurity, or helplessness in the child—are justified by the end (i.e., socially acceptable behavior). Respondents in the survey on spanking reported that even when they felt some guilt over spanking ("This hurts me more than it hurts you!"). Such parents define their parenting roles narrowly. When asked, they often cite the critical importance of raising their child "properly." What is proper is defined (implicitly, if not explicitly) by the culture within which one is immersed. However, ameaningful parenting occurs when parents extend their desire for social conformity to their children and punish them for failing to conform. As a result, when their child deviates from the "true" path, then they apply force to get him or her back into the socially approved "rut."

This exclusive focus on the rationale, rather than the effects of the disciplinary actions or the child's experience of them, is reflected most clearly in the absurdity of a parent hitting a child in order to teach him not to hit. The end result is immediate compliance by the child, but long-term damage to the child's ability to engage in independent moral reasoning—a necessary component of social and emotional competence (Goleman 1995; Grolnick, Deci, & Ryan 1997; Kochanska & Thompson 1997).

How did such ideas develop and become common childrearing practices? And why would they persist across generations of human families? Returning to our earlier motif, the answer is because they have value within the social and cultural groups to which humans belong. Conformity is the currency of most social systems. Individuals within a society are valued insofar as they embody and enact the shared values of the culture. Having value within the culture guarantees a higher level of acceptance, increasing the likelihood that the child will be nurtured by the group, including those outside the family (e.g., teachers, coaches, professors, scout leaders, etc.). Such external support both validates the parents' approach to childrearing and reduces the anxiety that the child will be ostracized, ignored, or otherwise neglected by the social group. The benefits to survival are self-evident. If a principal purpose of childrearing is the survival of one's genes into another generation, inculcating values that increase social standing and acceptance must play a central role in childrearing practices.

Toward a Model of Meaningful Parenting

Although these patterns of childrearing may increase social acceptability and enhance social standing, they also exact intra- and inter-personal costs. Learning to base relationships on power differentials, incorporating a belief that social conformity equals personal worth, and assuming that certain values must be inculcated, even if doing so damages the developing psychology of the recipient, creates a foundation from which moral cruelty may ensue. As Alice Miller (1983) points out, the consequences of this top-down approach reach beyond the family, effectively preparing the child for a lifetime of manipulation:

> The father receives his power from God (and from his own father). The teacher finds the soil already prepared for obedience, and the political leader has only to harvest what is sown. . . . As an adult, this child will often allow himself to be manipulated by various forms of propaganda since he is already used to having his 'inclinations' manipulated and has never known anything else (Miller 1983: 43-45).

When these assumptions underlie patterns of childrearing, they not only mask the harm done to children, but also virtually assure that the practices will continue. As long as the harm is not perceived it will endure. The task, then, is to challenge the hidden assumptions and automatic processing of implicit parenting rules that produce ameaningful moral systems and resultant moral cruelty. In this way what was concealed may become apparent.

To bring about basic changes in parenting we must first identify and separate the toxic assumptions that underlie harmful patterns of parenting from assumptions that promote healthy moral development. The most insidious of these toxic beliefs may be the belief that there exists only one way of being in the world, a straight and narrow path along which a child must be forcibly directed.

What alternative portrait of parenting might we paint? To answer that question as if there were one answer would itself reflect ameaningful thinking. As we saw in the previous chapter, Koch (1981) argues that life presents itself in an infinite variety of patterns, and thus the personal, integrative task remains a daunting one. A person committed to meaningful thought and meaningful moral reasoning must necessarily struggle with the gap between abstract principles and the particular, concrete events of life. Because this infinite variety of life events cannot, even in principle, be specified in advance, there can never exist a simple correspondence between formalized rule and concrete event. Once we acknowledge the infinite range of life events, each of which may be perceived from more than one perspective, then we begin to grasp the enormity of the parenting task. Just as "systems" can never bridge the gap between theory and life or integrate thought and action, they can likewise never offer one recipe for the raising of a child.

However, this does not mean that more effective parenting is not possible. Effective parenting seems to lie not in learning specific parenting techniques or content, but in facilitating the development of the child's self. Humility provides the essential context for meaningful parenting. Parenting strategies that minimize parental power, promote the child's sense of choice and feelings of self-determination, and include explanations for why a particular behavior or belief is valued enhance the development of independent moral reasoning (Kuczynski & Hildebrandt 1997). Or, as Simone Weil so eloquently expressed it, "The supernatural virtue of justice consists of behaving exactly as though there were equality when one is the stronger in an unequal relationship" (in Frost and Bell-Metereau 1998: 84).

In this dialogical system, rather than interacting on the basis of power, the parent relates to the child as a significant other, a manner of relating that Martin Büber (1970) termed an "I-Thou" relationship. For instance, instead of asking only, "What do I have to teach my child," one asks also, "What can I learn from my child?" Equally important, perhaps, is asking, "Who is this child," a question that conveys recognition of the child's autonomy and uniqueness. Returning to Alice Miller:

> Theoretically, I can imagine that someday we will regard our children not as creatures to manipulate or to change but rather as messengers from a world we once deeply knew, but which we have long since forgotten, who can reveal to us more about the true secrets of life, and also our own lives, than our parents were ever able to (1983: xi).

Daniel Goleman (1995) has reached similar conclusions in his research on emotional intelligence. A key component of emotional intelligence involves the development of empathy via attunement (Stern 1985). Attunement refers to those dialogical moments of intimacy wherein a child's expressions of emotion are understood and mirrored; the I-Thou relatedness of parent and child is manifest. It is important to understand that this mode of interaction cannot be faked. Attunement is not a "technique," but a way of relating. "If you just imitate a baby. . . , that only shows you know what he did, not how he felt. To let him know you sense how he feels, you have to play back his inner feelings in another way. Then the baby knows he is understood" (Goleman 1995: 100). Attunement fosters the emotive capabilities of child and parent, and both are enriched by the experience. Goleman (1995) contends that "the countlessly repeated moments of attunement or misattunement between parent and child shape the emotional expectations adults bring to their close relationships—perhaps far more than the more dramatic events of childhood" (1995: 100).

Once this is understood, obedience as the litmus test for "goodness" shows itself to be false. Goodness becomes a qualitative rendering, a goodness of fit between a child's own temperament and the decisions she makes daily, between a child's emotional experience and the empathic attunement of the parent. Instead of equating goodness with obedience, judgments of goodness are rendered in terms of identity, integrity, and character. A child who maintains this fidelity to self is on her way to establishing integrity of identity; thus she may gain the respect and admiration of others. Likewise, a parent who has nurtured with humility garners the respect of the child. Respect emerges as a consequence of reciprocity, of relatedness, rather than being bestowed on the basis of power.

To the extent that a healthy sense of identity, an integrity of self, and a capacity for critical thinking and meaningful moral reasoning develop within the crucible of empathic caring, then whenever it is lacking an opportunity for individuation is thwarted. Although the problem may seem to be an individual one, it is not. The social dimensions are of overwhelming import. This issue is not about individuality versus the communal good, but rather about how communities shape the individuals who comprise them. For example, when spontaneous expressions of delight are inhibited, learning as discovery diminishes and avoiding prohibitions becomes the primary goal of behavior. Naïve perceptions of reality give way to rule-mediated perceptions, and the natural language of the heart is lost to the rote language of social code. The individual fails to develop her own capacity for meaningful moral reasoning, to create her own moral narrative, adopting instead a prefabricated, socially sanctioned coda created by formulaic dispensation.

The level of moral cruelty that arises from individual ameaningful moral systems intensifies when these systems conspire to produce multiple, conflicting, and accidental priorities. The product is a failure to align life choices with a moral narrative of one's own making. One "should" undertake parenting, for example, but one "must" also succeed at one's career, be a model citizen in one's community, support one's community of faith, continue certain hobbies and recreational commitments, and so on. To the extent that these demands are experienced not simply as overlapping, but conflicting, and to the extent that they are seen as imposed rather than chosen, the potential for a "divided self" is great. Also, to the extent that a failure of critical thinking and meaningful moral reasoning provides the vehicle that transported us to this station, we encounter another powerful existential dilemma: How do we choose which track to take from the station, in what order, and to what destination?

Answering this question presupposes the very capacities that we lack—and the absence of which brought us to this point in the first place. It is often at precisely this juncture—where the capacity for critical thinking and meaningful moral reasoning leaves off—that pre-fabricated justifications fill in. Changing dearly held patterns of parenting is a grand goal; the argument for change subtle and complex. It lacks the appeal to emotion that often sustains existing patterns of power-based parenting and is greeted skeptically by many well-intentioned parents.

> But liberation from centuries of constraint can scarcely be expected to take place in a single generation. The idea that we as parents can learn more about the laws of life from a newborn child than we can from our parents will strike many older people as absurd and ridiculous (Miller 1983: 101).

Systemic changes of any kind are difficult to initiate and slow to proceed. However, the alternative of retaining the current system despite its glaring deficiencies and harmful results is not an acceptable answer either.

Chapter Four

Education: Lessons in Ameaning

with contributing author Susan Hanson

Medford High School, whatever its appearances, was not a school. It was a place where you learned to do—or were punished for failing in—a variety of exercises. The content of these exercises mattered not at all. What mattered was form, repetition, and form. . . . The process treated your mind as though it were a body part capable of learning a number of protocols, then repeating, repeating. If you'd done what you should have at Medford High, the transition into a factory, into an office, into the Marines would be something you'd barely notice; it would be painless. —Mark Edmundson

Schools didn't have to train kids to think they should consume nonstop, it simply taught them not to think at all. —John Taylor Gatto

Spring, 1958. Twenty-two first graders sit at their desks reading when, suddenly, a torrential rain begins to fall. Such storms are hardly unusual in this Texas Gulf Coast town, but the students are bored, and the downpour is far more interesting than another of Dick and Jane's tiresome adventures. Students run to the windows. For just a moment, all 22 children stand there, elbows propped on the windowsills, mesmerized by the rising water on the school's front lawn. Then the teacher speaks in a high, thin voice, "Children! Sit down! You've all seen rain before!"

Starting from this seemingly innocuous incident, we can begin to ask a fundamental question: What is the purpose of schooling? Not education, but compulsory schooling of the kind that dominates early 21st century American public education. Is it acquisition of the three R's? Is it to produce an educated citizenry? Or is it, as some have argued (Gatto 2003) to produce a compliant, standardized populace?

Returning to our opening example, certainly no one would argue against the need for a teacher to encourage students to remain on task. Teachers ourselves, we would never advance such an argument. Nonetheless, below the surface of this seemingly simple moment, we find a number of assumptions about authority and order, the goals of education, the value of mediated experience, and suppression of the active engagement that is a precursor to meaningful reasoning.

The preceding chapters have attempted to define the phenomenon of ameaningful morality, to establish its elements and likely outcomes, and to identify its developmental origins. However, if ameaningful moral systems operate throughout our society, then we would expect to find them at every level of cultural organization. Not merely isolated instances of such mechanisms, but social institutions wherein covert cruelty has become sacrament. Such a claim predicts an array of concentric circles, with ameaningful morality being inculcated first at the level of the parent-child dyad before proceeding to educational and cultural systems. Thus, we are able to imagine self-righteous parents "beating the hell" out of a child while seeing themselves as good parents, school principals delivering corporal punishment "for the child's own good," religious leaders calling for "holy" war—all creating and sustaining moral belief systems that are handmaidens to cruel desires.

It is our task, then, to examine the ways in which traditional methods of education may sustain ameaningful moral systems. In so doing, our guiding question is this: *How do standard educational models take energetic, curious 6 year-olds into one end of the educational pipeline, and turn out bored, incurious 18 year-olds at the other?*

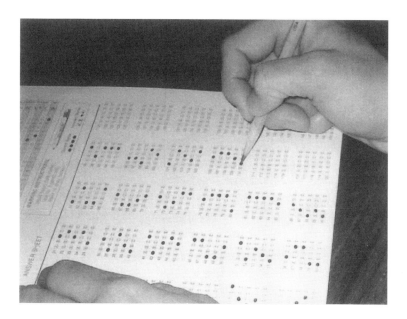

Returning again to the opening story, we must first examine the teacher's implicit rationale: Return order to the class. To the extent that a teacher's role entails creating an environment wherein focused, disciplined learning can occur, she did what seemed best for the class. However, implicit in this rationale are other, less obvious demands. To explore this point, let us examine a similar incident in which the seeds of ameaningful reasoning are more evident.

Consider a small group of first graders participating in an after-school program in a private home. They arrive by bus around three o'clock, have a snack, and then move to the living room where they are told to sit quietly and read or color for the next two hours. The children are complying with these directions when, suddenly, a fire engine roars by and stops at a house just down the block. Anxious to see what is happening, the children run to the window. Their caregiver, a woman who values order, rushes into the room and demands that all the children, including her own, sit down. "That is nothing that concerns you!" she yells to the children. Obediently, they take their seats and sit in silence for the remainder of the afternoon.

To unveil the belief structures that underlie such commonplace incidents, it is essential to begin with observations about the developing child. At this age (say six or so), a child is developing a sense of ego mastery, a sense of her own competence. Consequently, information becomes increasingly important to her. Knowing how to do things constitutes an important source of self-confidence and pride. Although her cognitive abilities have developed significantly, they have yet to evolve fully. "There are still some limitations on thinking, since the child is reliant on the immediate environment and has difficulty with abstract ideas. . . . What the child at this stage cannot do is speculate abstractly or use deductive logic" (Smith, Cowie & Blades 1998: 295). Simply put, the six-year-old lives more in a world of sensory *things* than a world of abstract ideas. Knowing the world means seeing it, touching it, *engaging* it in an intimate, physical way. Cognitive knowledge and the sense of mastery that ensues from such knowledge stem largely from active, uninhibited exploration of the world.

Maria Montessori, Alfred Adler, and Rudolf Steiner all constructed educational models based on this model of childhood development. As David Sobel (1993) explains, as a person develops, his world expands to meet his changing needs. Rather than unfolding in a lock-step sequence of discrete developmental steps, childhood development "should be considered as a series of spheres, with the earlier matrixes contained within each subsequent one. Each matrix is the significant world, or the safe place in which the individual resides" (1993: 54). For the infant or the very young child, that "safe place" is ideally the mother, the father, the family, the home. By the age of six or seven however, the child is ready to venture farther out, to explore the world of things, even as the quality of early parenting, of attunement (see Chapter 3), sets an upper limit on this preparedness. As Sobel puts it,

> The unquenchable appetite for the out-of-doors that many children show at this age is an indicator of the move into the earth matrix. Pearce's use of the term "earth matrix" refers broadly to the actual stuff of the concrete world—trees, dirt, animals, and plants of the natural world, as well as pencils, houses, clothes and the human made things of the world. As

> Piaget contends that appropriate learning is through the actual
> stuff of the world, Pearce contends that it is in this world that
> children start to feel at home (1993: 58).

Drawing on the results of several studies, Gordon Hale (1979) begins with what may seem an obvious conclusion: "With increasing age and/or level of intelligence there is an increase in amount of stimulus information to which children attend in discriminating among learning stimuli" (1979: 48). In short, older students are more capable of selectively attending to specific stimuli, the sheer number of stimuli notwithstanding. As Hale points out, however, this truth is neither as simple nor as obvious as it seems.

> In theoretical analyses of attention development, much
> emphasis has been placed on the idea that young children
> attend to a wide range of information in the stimulus and that
> with maturity, children become increasingly more selective.
> Yet evidence from the component selection research discussed
> here seems to indicate that as children develop, they become
> less rather than more selective, attending to an increasing
> amount of stimulus information. To understand this apparent
> discrepancy, it is important to bear in mind the distinction
> between children's ability to exercise selectivity and their
> disposition to do so. . . Where children's natural disposition
> is concerned, there is a developmental trend, not toward
> greater selectivity but toward increasingly broader attention
> deployment (1979: 48-49).

While a six-year-old may wish to attend to a single stimulus, she possesses a limited *capacity* to selectively choose from multiple stimuli. Conversely, as children grow older, they are increasingly *capable* of selecting and attending to a single stimulus chosen from various competing stimuli. Simply stated, extended attention to a specific stimulus requires a mindset that deviates from the cognitive abilities of the young child. Why then do we ask children to do something that, according to maturational timetables, they are not yet capable of doing? To address this question we must first ask what the consequences are for: (1) requiring something of a child that she is not capable of doing (paying attention to a single stimulus for a long period of time); (2) ignoring a child's innate curiosity and desire to know the physical world (refusing to let her witness a firetruck in action); and (3) implicitly invalidating a child's urge to discover by rendering the desire "inappropriate" (demanding that children sit down because the fire is "none of their business").

Regardless of the intentions of the teacher, it is our contention that the pedagogical push to preserve order by demanding that children suppress intrinsic needs to discover their world suppresses meaningful thinking. As Koch so eloquently described it, "in meaningful thinking, the mind caresses, flows joyously into, over, around the relational matrix defined by the problem, the object" (Koch 1981: 79). Every action of an educator that quashes this innate curiosity simultaneously inhibits the intrinsic motivation that lies at the core of authentic learning. As Simone Weil said, "the intelligence can only be led by desire.... The joy of learning is as indispensable in study as breathing is in running. Where it is lacking there are no real students, but only poor caricatures of apprentices who, at the end of their apprenticeship, will not even have a trade" (in Frost and Bell-Metereau 1998: 54). This pedagogical strategy conceals a moral lesson as well. By reducing a child to an object to be manipulated, or shaped, an I-It style of relating displaces an I-Thou style (to use Büber's terminology).

A Consumption/Production Model of Education

Another facet of modern education that contributes to the development and maintenance of ameaningful reasoning involves the standardized production model employed in many schools. Indeed, we often refer to someone as a "product" of a given school. On one level, we employ the term colloquially to indicate the institution at which a person developed a particular set of skills, as in "basketball great Tim Duncan is a product of Wake Forest University." In a more serious vein, this language points to our tendency to think of students as commodities to be prepared for the job market—products by which educational institutions will be judged. Higher test scores, a higher number of graduates going on to college, a higher percentage of young men and women finding work in their chosen fields—these are the marks of a successful educational institution, the signs that a high quality product has been milled. Commendable as some of these outcomes may be, the criteria themselves have evolved from a model that conceals serious flaws. In his critique of Upton Sinclair s *The Goslings: A Study of American Schools*, H.L. Mencken describes the nature of this flaw:

> That erroneous assumption is to the effect that the aim of public education is to fill the young of the species with knowledge and awaken their intelligence, and make them fit to discharge the duties of citizenship in an enlightened and independent manner. Nothing could be further from the truth.
>
> The aim of public education is not to spread enlightenment at all; it is simply to reduce as many individuals as possible to the same safe level, to breed and train a standardized citizenry, to down dissent and originality. That is its aim in the United States, whatever the pretensions of politicians, pedagogues and other such mountebanks, and that is its aim everywhere else (Mencken 1924 in *The American Mercury*).

The image of students as products reinforces this aim. It implies *passivity* on the part of the students and connotes their *completion*—as well as a standard of success based on uniformity, utility, and delimited performance parameters. It assumes that what the student is learning is quantifiable, and that the quality of this product is equivalent to a quantitative score. Finally, it implies a correlative criterion of "return on investment." Only that which offers a good return is a worthy and wise investment. To the extent that the demands of modern life are no longer rooted in an industrial economic model, approaching education in this way no longer fits the organizational reality into which students eventually emerge (cf. Toffler 1980).

Even while criticizing current models, recent education reformers still cling to the core assumptions of the production model. In making their case for a different approach to education, brothers Robert and Jon Solomon state:

The argument that the university is an 'investment' in the
future and should make a contribution to the surrounding
community sounds great to legislators and local taxpayers.
But the notion of investment slips from the legitimate concern
for the future of the community to the narrow, destructive
emphasis on short-term returns. The real interests of
students and the community get sacrificed to an overly
restricted commodity and production model. It does not
allow for perhaps the single most important fact about an
education, and that is how much searching and reflection,
how many false starts and wrong roads, how much 'waste'
an education often requires. A decent education includes any
number of 'useless,' 'impractical' subjects as well as skills
with some—we hope—immediate application, and that means
that the very idea of the university as an investment institution
is in error (1993: 17).

Echoing this critique, Joseph Peel and C.E. McCary (1997) call
for a new language, a new metaphor for schooling. But unlike Robert
and Jon Solomon, they see the problem as a purely pragmatic one. The
underlying assumptions of a product orientation are no longer even
relevant to the skills and attributes essential for success in the modern
workplace.

The most familiar features of the traditional factory—a
hierarchical authority system, layers of bureaucracy,
breaking work down into meaningless small pieces, telling
people precisely what to do, controlling people through rules
and policies that fit every situation—have simply proved
inadequate as ways to get people to produce high-quality
work (1997: 698).

Peel and McCary suggest reconceptualizing schools as
"knowledge-work organizations." They view the student "as a worker
in the organization who helps produce knowledge; the teacher [as] a leader
of these workers; the principal [as] the CEO of the organization" (1997:
699). The product in this new paradigm is *not* what the student learns
and accomplishes, but rather something that Peel and McCary refer to as
"knowledge work." Extending the metaphor, they write, "we believe that

schools have both internal and external customers. In addition to being knowledge workers, students are the primary internal customers because they must buy (i.e., agree to do) the work that teachers design for them. The external customers of schools are the society in general and employers and parents in particular." As "stockholders" in the organization, taxpayers not only finance the organization, but also hold it accountable for producing high quality "knowledge work" (Peel & McCary 1997: 698).

How does this paradigm differ from the old consumption and production model? Cloaked in the language of Total Quality Management, this "new design" still shares a basic premise with its predecessor. The goal of education is to create a product. The language has changed, but the underlying reality remains unscathed. Once again, we encounter the chameleon–like nature of ameaningful thought: The obvious intentions of the system appear neutral, helpful even, while the underlying assumptions promulgate the continuing objectification of others and their resultant maltreatment.

But what if production was *not* the goal of education? What if the real objective was something less tangible, but more difficult to assess? In *The Courage to Teach*, Parker Palmer asserts that "to educate is to guide students on an inner journey toward more truthful ways of seeing and being in the world" (1998: 6). It is, he maintains, an activity built on a relationship of mutuality (or attunement), a relationship that binds the knower to the known. For this idea, Palmer is clearly indebted to Martin Büber.

> The experience of It is planned and purposeful. Yet the man who experiences It does not go out of himself to do so, and the It does not respond but passively allows itself to be experienced. The Thou, on the other hand, cannot be sought, for it meets one through grace. Yet the man who knows Thou must go out to meet the Thou and step into direct relation with it, and the Thou responds to the meeting (Friedman 1960: 58-59).

What the teacher must offer the student, then, is not simply a set of propositions or facts, an "It" to which that student can relate objectively, but a subject, a "Thou" with which the student can *interact*. As Palmer puts it, "When we know the other as a subject, we do not merely hold it at arm's length. We know it in and through relationship . . ." (1998: 102-103). A student enters into such a union by being drawn in by another human being. By relating to the teacher as a self (a Thou), the student enters into that teacher's love for her subject, and is thereby engaged himself.

If this process sounds impractical, or perhaps even mystical, it is because the exchange is taking place not between an "I" and an "It," but among a trio of living selves—the student, the teacher, and the text. "[I]n a subject-centered classroom, the teacher's central task is to give the great thing an independent voice—a capacity to speak its truth quite apart from the teacher's voice in terms that students can hear and understand" (Palmer 1998: 118). The goal of education in this model is not to produce a product—whether that product be a body of knowledge, a more perfect student, or a sterling reputation for the school. Rather, the goal is to create a relationship between a student and a lived truth. In undertaking this great venture, both student and teacher engage themselves in an open-ended *process*, or, as Palmer puts it, a never-ending journey toward the truth.

The Battle for Power and the Language of Siege

Another locus of concern in the modern educational model lies in the assumption that education is, at its heart, a struggle of wills—the students struggling against the teacher and the teacher controlling the students. To examine this issue, consider another life example. A student sat on the very front row, arms folded close against her chest, eyes piercing through the lectern straight into the teacher's heart. Or so it seemed. Three mornings a week, this student attended class without fail. Wearing a perpetual scowl and slumping in her desk as though she'd lost her energy for life, she seldom said a word. On those rare occasions when she did, it was invariably to challenge something that the teacher had said. Young and terrified, the novice instructor took each of those challenges as a personal affront. Saving face before the class became her primary concern, and to do that she realized that she had to reclaim her power.

We would like to be able to report that this student and instructor finally came to terms, or that they gradually closed the distance between teacher and learner. However, they did not. Granted, they did reach a rapprochement of sorts by the end of the semester, but the instructor never ceased to see the student as a threat. She guarded her power well. Confrontations of this sort are inevitable in education. Indeed, they are expected. In marked contrast, we argue that the battle for power is one of the most insidious sources of ameaning in the classroom. Masked by the legitimate desire for order, discipline, and safety, the need to transform the classroom from a crucible of learning into a dominion of power plays itself out in myriad ways. All these ways produce unintended "ends" that are antithetical to cultivating character, refining critical thinking, or perpetuating meaningful moral reasoning.

Where does this leave us? Are we to pretend that the need for order in the classroom is misplaced, or worse, subtly sadistic? Are we recommending that respect and authority are antiquated notions from another age? In short, no. Just as Alice Miller observed in her writings on parenting, challenging abusive patterns of control does not mean "children should be raised without restraints." Incivility and inattention are no more likely to lead to a meaningful educational structure than rigid demands for compliance and control. The issue becomes one of how to achieve an environment that includes appropriate limits, yet facilitates exploration. Because the two polarities have opposite pulls, this goal involves an inherent tension—a complex paradox. It is into this tension that we must bring a keen moral acuity.

In our opening chapter we declared that ameaningful morality involves two distinct but interrelated components: (1) The internalization of moral rules that excuse harm against certain others under certain conditions; and (2) The development of cognitive processes that evoke automatic, non-conscious application of these moral codes rather than activating independent moral reasoning. Exploring the consumption/ production model of education and the battle of wills many educators see at the core of teaching, we discover both of these components. The one-size-fits-all approach of the consumption/production model reduces students to an "It," depriving them of the status necessary to engage in learning as a dynamic, emergent process. By conveying to students that their worth is as a product, that their meaning within the educational system is defined by their performance on standardized exams and accomplishments after their schooling is completed, we justify the harm that ensues from ignoring the humanity of our students and suppressing their natural curiosity. Students, for their part, are repeatedly conditioned to view themselves (and others) as mere products, valued for their achievements rather than their inquisitiveness, and the "organic determination of the form and substance of thought" that defines meaningful thought is gradually destroyed (Koch 1981: 79). The result is a line of donkeys, walking the same narrow rut, proceeding toward the same narrow goal (increasingly defined as performance on a standardized test).

When educators come to view the classroom as a battleground where the imposition of their wills is a necessary precondition for learning, the second component required for developing and sustaining ameaningful moral systems falls into place. As with parenting, an authoritarian stance toward children shifts the child's attention away from personal experiencing to an end-justifies-the-means mentality in which the prescriptive definition of "good" supercedes the value of individuals. In the wake of these authoritarian interactions we find students given to mindless application of learned rules. They are discouraged from the active thinking and genuine engagement with the subject matter that are prerequisites for meaningful reasoning.

As obedience supplants mindful inquiry as the basis for the child's developing sense of morality, it also becomes the singular measure of "good" behavior. Children internalize a learning model characterized by an unthinking, unfeeling acceptance of what others tell them to believe. Having failed to learn to think for themselves, they struggle to initiate independent reasoning across multiple domains, reacting to moral dilemmas as if they were taking a multiple-choice exam and striving to identify the memorized answer without having to know *why it represents a desired outcome*.

The Capacity for Paradox

"Teaching and learning require a higher degree of awareness than we ordinarily possess—and awareness is always heightened when we are caught in a creative tension. Paradox is another name for that tension, a way of holding opposites together that creates an electric charge that keeps us awake" (Palmer 1998: 74). Palmer's view of paradox runs counter to what most people assume is necessary for education to occur. To many, education is about acquiring information, and developing practical skills. Granted, education *is* about these things, but it is not *only* about these things. It is also about what we cannot know, about doubts and questions, and about the limits of human thought. At its best, learning is a risky business, an undertaking fraught with tension and marked by unpredictable twists and turns. Authentic education should make us tremble.

Fear is a natural response when one moves from a closed to an open-ended system. Familiar fixed structures that contain us—rules, goals, chains of command—also make us feel secure. Consequently, our first reaction when we believe that the familiar rules are under attack is to assume a posture of defense. This tendency may be seen not only in home and school, but in the workplace as well—an arena to which we turn in the next chapter. "Some organizations defend themselves superbly even against their employees with regulations, guidelines, time clocks, and policies and procedures for every eventuality" (Wheatley 1994: 16). "One organization I worked in welcomed its new employees with a list of twenty-seven offenses for which they would be summarily fired—and the assurance that they could be fired for other reasons as well" (Wheatley 1994: 16-17).

Ironically, when maintaining the system—or protecting authority—becomes the overriding goal, the system begins to die. When the relationship between student and teacher is marked by fear and distrust, the relationship withers. We have two models then, or perhaps, two poles of an organizational continuum: A fixed, closed system in which the goals are safety, efficiency, and control; and a pliable, open system in which the driving goal is a relationship with truth. Unlike the first system, which is static, the second is very much alive. Where there is life, there are paradoxes and uncertainties. Stir up a bare patch of soil, and in time, a seedling will rise from the earth. Burn a stand of jack pines, and hundreds of new saplings will emerge. What looks like random destruction may, in time, crystallize as patterned renewal. What looks like chaos may be the process of change—new patterns in the making.

Looking back over his own career as a teacher, Parker Palmer writes that every class ultimately involves relatedness as its core. "The techniques I have mastered do not disappear, but neither do they suffice. Face to face with my students, only one resource is at my immediate command: my identity, my selfhood, my sense of this 'I' who teaches— without which I have no sense of the 'Thou' who learns" (Palmer 1998: 10). Ultimately, Palmer says, "we teach who we are" (1998: 2), and it is "who we are" that gives us real authority. "Power works from the outside in, but authority works from the inside out" (1998: 32). True authority "is granted to people perceived as *authoring* their own words, their own actions, their own lives, rather than playing a scripted role at great remove from their own hearts" (1998: 33). The real educator, it would seem, operates at the opposite end of the control spectrum. She seeks not to control the lives of her students, but rather to enable them to author their own lives. Real authority, and by extension, real morality, lies not in our power, but in our humanity, the very thing that also makes us weak. It is from this vantage that we are most likely to embrace the full spectrum of human reality—feeling and intellect, freedom and discipline, chaos and order, flexibility and stability, insecurity and safety.

Chapter Five

Ameaning and the Workplace

*Annual income twenty pounds, annual expenditure nineteen
pounds and six, result happiness. Annual income twenty pounds,
annual expenditure twenty pounds ought and six, result misery.*
—*Charles Dickens*

A few years ago, I (TLH) attended a meeting in which a managing
partner of a large consulting firm informed his employees that recent
layoffs had been done "in the individuals' best interest" (they would turn
out to be the first in a series of layoffs that is now entering its fifth year).
By his account, it was unfair for the company to continue to employ
persons with outdated skill sets, because it prevented them from finding
other jobs in which their skills might be useful. It would also, he claimed,
prevent them from obtaining the re-training they would need to improve
their value in the marketplace. Everyone in attendance knew that there
were no other jobs in which an outdated skill set had value, yet no one
lodged the slightest appeal. To paraphrase Pink Floyd, hanging on in quiet
desperation is the workers' way.

Many other examples of cruelty and quiet acquiescence in the
workplace are available from the most obviously outrageous (e.g., the

treatment of migrant farm workers and immigrant sweatshop workers), to the subtle (e.g., forced early retirement and age discrimination, or accounting fraud that robs retirees of their pensions) are possible. The goal however, is not to catalog all of the injustices that occur in organizational life; rather, it is to start us thinking about the origins of a tacit pledge of allegiance to an organizational ideology that relies on power and domination (the two key ingredients in morally cruel behavior) to sustain itself.

When applying the concept of ameaningful morality to the workplace, we must first examine the specific beliefs that underlie our understanding of employment. It is not ameaningful thinking per se that lies at the heart of workplace cruelty, although here too rule-bound, automatic cognitive processes play their role. Rather it is in the application of specific ameaningful rules developed within family and educational systems that the moral cruelty evident in modern organizational life resides.

Ameaningful moral systems, created when authoritarian parents instill intolerant moral systems that contain prohibitions against questioning, facilitate the automaticity that is the essence of ameaningful moral reasoning. The fruits of these moral systems ripen in traditional educational systems and are harvested when, as adults, we embrace a workplace culture that at once both nurtures these beliefs and exploits them. It is here that the operation of ameaningful moral systems becomes so effective, so subtle that it is nearly undetectable. While overt acts of moral cruelty certainly occur in organizations, it is shared beliefs about authority and economic value that provide the fertile medium for the much more common covert acts of cruelty to flourish.

Ameaningful Work

If we analyze the usual role of the individual in the workplace, organizational life becomes a series of defining myths and descriptive metaphors that are, in fact, the building blocks of a shared organizational ideology. This ideology, embodied in the top-down organizational hierarchies that dominate 21st century American business, has been characterized as a form of *psychic prison* (Morgan 1997). Both organizational life and prisons are inherently constraining. What Morgan (1997) deftly illustrates is how we create hierarchical dominance systems within institutions that then dominate us—all the while failing to perceive how or why we constructed our own prison.

The power of the psychic prison derives from its ability to prevent us from seeing it as constraining. Hidden within the Trojan horse of success lie tacit assumptions about our role in organizations and our place in the power hierarchies that define them. Having learned the top-down language of domination at home and school, we become unable to perceive our lives within society and its institutions from any other vantage. Growing up within a dominance hierarchy produces attributes ideally suited to the needs of the organizational machine.

> If we examine the history of work organization since the beginning of the Industrial Revolution, we find a common pattern in both Europe and North America. The development of a system of wage labor tends to be followed by increasingly strict and precise organization, close supervision, and increasingly standardized jobs. Skilled and semiskilled workers are increasingly replaced by cheaper unskilled workers, leading to what is sometimes described as 'degradation' or 'deskilling' of work and 'homogenization' of the labor market (Morgan 1997: 312).

Working to survive has not always entailed a structure of dominance; in fact, working for others is a fairly modern development. For the centuries prior to the Industrial Revolution, the nuclear family was the unit of production. Between 1760 and 1850 the percentage of self-employed laborers in the US remained steady, hovering around 80%; however, with the onset of the Industrial Revolution, the picture changed dramatically. By 1860, 52% of workers were self-employed, but by 1900 that number had dropped to 35.4%. In 1980, the percentage of the population who was self-employed was 10.8%, and by 2000 that number had dropped to 7.9% (Edwards, Reich, and Weisskopf: 1986; U.S. Department of Labor website: www.dol.gov/dol/library.htm).

This change has created a new kind of servitude, one in which the worker *cum* servant becomes an integral participant in maintaining the system that ensnares him. Workers' value is determined by their contribution to corporate profits. Downsizing (or, in its more current euphemism, "rightsizing") has made painfully apparent the role workers play in modern corporate life.

> The worker sells his person and his liberty for a given time. The worker is in the position of a serf because this terrible threat of starvation which daily hangs over his head and over his family, will force him to accept any conditions imposed by the gainful calculations of the capitalist, the industrialist, the employer. [T]he worker always has the right to leave his employer, but has he the means to do so? No, he does it in order to sell himself to another employer. He is driven to it by the same hunger which forces him to sell himself to the first employer. Thus, the worker's liberty. . . is only a theoretical freedom, lacking any means for its possible realisation, and consequently it is only a fictitious liberty, an utter falsehood (Bakunin 1964: 187).

Nonetheless, we willingly occupy our places in these organizations, plowing the very ground in which moral cruelty may take root.

> [W]e are conduits for the enterprises in which we participate. Ideas pass through us, spirituality and certainly the desire for money passes through us as certainly as the cord through the wooden hands of a marionette. When large corporations are the ultimate purveyors of what we make, it has to affect our work. We become conduits for corporate ideology. We take the check and wonder why we're miserable (Bogosian 1999: www.ericbogosian.com/letter23.html).

If we are to fully understand this phenomenon, we must be able to perceive exactly what we are giving up—time with a spouse or significant other, time with our children or friends, time spent cultivating interests or hobbies, time engaged in those social activities that bind us to one another. We surrender our autonomy and self-determination, our spontaneity and creativity, and our sense of connection to the whole. In its stead, we accept employment as the basis for our sense of belonging as much as for the material wealth it provides. Corporate culture replaces community culture in an age when belonging to traditional communities has been made increasingly difficult due, in large part, to the demands of our employers. Note how similar the conflicts created by these systems are to those compiled by Moustakas in his description of the effects of domination-based child-rearing practices (Chapter 3): alienation, loneliness, loss of spontaneity, muting of self-identity, external compliance and manipulation, and denial of choice. What is sown at home and school is systematically reaped by organizations.

Misconceptions of the Modern Workplace

In a related take on the organization as psychic prison, theologian and social theorist Walter Wink spoke of collectives that constrain as "domination systems." Addressing their underlying structure, he wrote, "We become complicit. And so we leave unopposed the world that injures us, restructuring ourselves to appease the Powers we depend upon. To achieve peace within the world, we declare war upon ourselves" (1992: 42). In piercing the veil of domination systems, Wink discovered a substructure of toxic myths uncannily similar to those discussed in the previous chapters on Parenting and Education: (1) the belief that working hard will result in becoming rich; (2) a corollary assumption that money is of great value and its possession produces happiness; (3) the belief that production of skilled, employable people is of greater urgency than cultivation of character and promotion of healthy relationships; (4) the assumption that the perpetuation of order and prevention of chaos necessarily require a hierarchy of domination; and (5) a valuing and rewarding those who manage or control over those who provide labor.

In order to examine further the specific assumptions that facilitate the creation of ameaningful workplaces, we must examine each of Wink's assumptions (and the relation of each to the ameaningful moral systems that underlie our beliefs about organizational structures) individually.

Assumption #1: Working hard will result in becoming rich (the "Horatio Alger" myth). If you work hard, you will become rich. This seems simple (and fair) enough. Hard work is rewarded; laziness is not. Those who work hard deserve the rewards that follow. Those who do not deserve the poverty they inhabit. This reasoning defines straightforward, empowering meritocracy at its best.

So, how does this simple notion create organizational systems that foster moral cruelty? The magic happens as we move from the myth of rugged individualism to the collective crucible within which our worklife is forged. Those who lead organizations, typically, are those whose work has been deemed the most profitable. As such, they are to be honored for two reasons. First, they have earned their positions in the hierarchy. Second, because they create wealth, what's good for them is good for us. In that the goal of work is, after all, wealth, those who create wealth must occupy the first ranks of society. Work equals rank, rank equals power.

There is at least one fatal flaw in this logic: Work does not equal rank; indeed, it never has. If we created a replacement slogan based on the actualities of social mobility, it would read more like, "If you are born rich you will probably stay rich." The following data illustrates the point: 95 percent of the 179 wealthiest executives and financiers in America at the turn of the century came from upper-class or upper-middle-class backgrounds (as did 86 percent of the United States Congress). Fewer than 5 percent started as poor immigrants or farm children (Miller 1949).

In order to camouflage the reality of wealth begetting wealth, "rags to riches tales" are constantly reinvented for the masses (the film, *Pretty Woman*, to cite one popular example), and the belief in a level economic playing field becomes a mantra. Concurrently, the same persons who benefit most from the current system expend their energies (and money) attempting to abolish the inheritance tax. While publicly professing faith in rugged individualism and in "pulling oneself up by the bootstraps," the frenetic efforts to transfer wealth and privilege to "one's own" conveys more clearly than words what lurks below the professed ideals.

Still, what is the harm in teaching people that hard work will be rewarded? From our perspective, it is harmful to the extent that it perpetuates dominance systems that create and sustain morally cruel behavior. It is harmful to the extent that it minimizes the likelihood of any reasonable discussion of social inequities and concentration of power (and wealth) in the same, small number of hands. It is harmful when well-intentioned, hard-working men and women wake one day to realize that much of their lives has been spent in vain pursuit of unobtainable goals.

Assumption #2: Money is of great value and its possession results in happiness.

The belief that the acquisition of material wealth and the accumulation of material goods constitute the road to a happy life is a cornerstone of the American value system. This belief is so deeply held that challenging it often provokes incredulous stares or accusations of treason. However, like the other misconceptions that we have examined, this one too hides another, more sinister face.

From Socrates to Locke, an overarching concern in our efforts to understand human happiness has been how to avoid mistaking imaginary happiness for the real thing. The search inevitably leads to one of two conclusions: (1) There exists a "true" form of happiness and, thus, pursuing false happiness produces rotten fruit—discord, sickness, death; or (2) Happiness is relative, reflecting a commitment to what is pleasurable; therefore, no distinction between "false" and "real" happiness is possible. The latter, more pragmatic of these philosophical positions has held sway since at least the 19th century and remains at the heart of the modern assumption that the acquisition of material comforts will lead to personal happiness. But what of the former notion? Can we judge the pursuit of happiness in terms of its outcomes?

We (that is to say inhabitants of industrialized, Western nations) live in a time of unprecedented luxury. We enjoy creature comforts beyond anything that previous generations could have imagined. But are we happier? Although Inglehart (1990) found a positive correlation between the wealth of a nation and the happiness of its citizens, he also found that the Germans and Japanese, despite having more than twice the GNP of Ireland, reported much lower levels of happiness than the Irish. Studies in the United States have found that greater income does not predict greater happiness (Diener, Horwitz, & Emmons 1985), nor does winning the lottery (Brickman, Coates, & Janoff-Bulman 1978). And, despite real increases in personal income in the last 30 years, the percentage of the population describing themselves as "very happy" has remained unchanged (Myers 1993).

Mihaly Csikszentmihalyi (1999) takes the analysis of the relation-ship between happiness and materialism even further. Synthesizing a large body of research, he identifies three reasons why material rewards fail to make us happy. First, rapid escalation of expectations constantly re-levels the playing field. As people reach the level of affluence they thought would make them happy, they quickly become habituated to that new baseline and begin longing for even higher levels of affluence. Second, when resources are distributed unequally (as they are throughout the modern world), people evaluate their material needs in comparison with those around them, rather than in terms of what they need to live. The discrepancy between what we have and what others have creates unhappiness. Third, while wealth may be rewarding in itself, happiness is comprised of several factors unrelated to money or possessions. Having a fulfilling family life, valued friendships, and outside interests have all been shown to be powerful predictors of happiness. While there is no necessary reason why pursuit of material rewards should preclude happiness in other areas, the reality is that the acquisition of money requires so much of our time that other pursuits become secondary and, therefore, less likely to be attained.

This line of reasoning probably comes as no great surprise. Like your mother may have told you, money cannot buy happiness. So, why then, do we as a society consistently place the accumulation of material wealth above all other goals, in deed if not in word? Here we see the reality of the psychic prison: We are so immersed in a misguided myth of our own making that we fail to see how we maintain our own prison. Even more troubling is the prospect that we accept the walls as necessary, the dominance hierarchy as holy, and the goals as desirable.

Assumption #3: The production of skilled, employable people is of greater urgency than the cultivation of character and promotion of healthy relationships.
That this maxim is widely held is evident in the changing face of college education. Those who perceive college as a training ground for the workforce and those who champion a broad liberal arts education are engaged in a desperate struggle. The former insist that college should serve as a kind of sophisticated vocational training for the highly technical, highly profitable jobs that await graduates in this new millennium. The latter, more traditional approach, insists that broadly educated students, trained primarily in critical thinking and writing skills, are best positioned to meet the myriad of life challenges and ethical decisions that lie ahead.

The "vocationalists" are winning. New technology programs abound. Computer Science and Information Technology are now among the most popular majors, rivaling even business administration as the top choice of today's students. While no one can argue that such training has value, the disagreement about whether vocational training or education for character will lead us to desired social ends remains.

A traditional liberal arts education, or "humanities education" as it is sometimes called, emphasizes the social, artistic, and human context within which life is lived. Students are required to take numerous art and literature courses, math and science courses, history, foreign language, and social science courses. The goal is a graduate broadly familiar with human culture.

The newer, technology-oriented curricula are altogether different. Because the technical skills they seek to impart are so demanding, little time is left for reading great fiction or studying classical Greek philosophy. They are designed to develop employable skills rather than character, to produce technicians rather than citizens. The result is an increasing number of college graduates who have never been exposed to the great ideas of humanity, never studied human behavior or social issues, never learned that science is a philosophy or that history is a perspective. Thus, those earmarked to be the leaders of the future may emerge poorly equipped to consider the human realities of life, more comfortable as they are with technology and cyber-life.

Assumption #4: The perpetuation of order and prevention of chaos necessarily require a hierarchy of domination.

The hidden trick in this assumption is to confuse authority with domination. Domination is, by definition, degrading. Authority—at least non-arbitrary, freely chosen authority—need not be. If we mistakenly assume that authority requires domination, then we become perfectly conditioned not only to tolerate morally cruel organizations, but even to *value* them.

Dominance hierarchies perpetuate a pyramidal power structure that concentrates power at or near the top—where only a select few reside. Promotion into the upper ranks is strictly controlled by those already there, usually requiring loyalty to a shared set of values as much as demonstrated leadership capacities. By way of a weeding out promotion philosophy, those with undesirable values may be let go alongside those with inferior skills.

For example, consider the performance review rating system used by General Electric, Ford, and the now defunct energy trading company, Enron. In this system managers rank employees against each other on a bell curve, assigning a certain, predetermined percentage of workers an "A" grade, the next percent a "B" grade, and so on. Such subjective rating systems inevitably create unfairness, based as they are on managers' own biases about the qualities the corporation (and the manager) values. "Moreover, the grading systems pit employees against each other, undermining teams, which are often intentionally put together with varying talents in mind. In Internet chat rooms, scores of employees complain they've been graded unfairly, feel angry and unappreciated, and don't want to collaborate with co-workers with higher grades" (Carol Hymowitz, *The Wall Street Journal Interactive Edition*, May 15, 2001: http://online.wsj.com/public/us).

In this zero-sum game, resources are artificially limited to create the illusion of scarcity (and, hence, value). If the masquerade is successful, those "lower" on the pyramid will gladly engage in all manner of cruel behavior, including rank-obtaining, self-promoting and career-building—all on the backs of others. As Morgan observes, "Domination . . . occurs. . . when a ruler imposes his or her will on others *while being perceived as having a right to do so.* . . . [F]orms of domination become legitimized as normal, socially acceptable power relations: patterns of formal authority in which rulers see themselves as having the right to rule, and those subject to this rule see it as their *duty* to obey" (1997: 304). This implicit, and accepted, struggle for domination lies at the core of modern organizational life.

Organizational cruelty may therefore be systemic, but it is individuals, emboldened by their place in the system, who give it agency. Domination is institutionalized and bureaucratized in modern organizational structures, allowing morally cruel behavior to flourish in relative anonymity. As Mouzelis noted, "Domination, when exercised over a large number of people, necessitates an administrative staff which will execute commands and which will serves as a bridge between the ruler and the ruled" (Mouzelis 1968: 16).

Weber's political sociology characterizes this organizational style as "legal domination." Power is concentrated in the hands of leaders who come to hold their positions through legal procedures (appointment, elections, etc.). The relations between leader and led are strictly defined by a shared set of impersonal rules that are enforced by a bureaucracy.

Assumption #5: Those who manage or control others have greater value, and deserve greater rewards, than those who provide labor.

In 1980, the average salary for a CEO of a major American corporation was 42 times greater than the pay of the typical American worker. By 1990, the ratio had more than doubled to 85 times the average worker's wage. As of 1998, that ratio was an incredible 419 times (*Business Week*, Special report: Executive pay, April 19, 1999). In 1998 alone the average American CEO salary jumped 36%, compared with 3.9% for the average white-collar worker and 2.7% for the average blue-collar worker. Consider this: The median annual family income in the United States in 1998 was $38,885. If the median family income increased at the same rate as the average CEO salary, in 5 years that family would earn $203,124. In 10 years, that same family would be earning an astounding $772,268 (*AFL-CIO*, November 18, 1999).

What are we to make of this trend? Could one not argue that these increases in CEO salaries simply reflect market forces at work? Are not these CEOs simply being compensated for the value they add to an organization (in improved profitability, increased stock prices, and the like)? The data suggest otherwise. In 1998 the average CEO in the United Kingdom made US $645,540 per year, the average CEO compensation in Japan was US $ 420,855, and the average annual CEO compensation in Germany was US $398,430. These figures contrast markedly with the United States average of $10,600,000. Unless we are willing to accept the completely unsubstantiated claim that the United States is suffering from a dire shortage of capable executives, we are left wondering.

But what of the "added value" argument? Again, let us examine the data. As noted above, the salary increase for United States CEOs rose 36% in 1998. During that same year, the average earnings for the companies piloted by these same CEOs *fell* 1.4%. The 36% figure also outpaced the stock performance of their companies, which rose 26.7% in 1998 (*Business Week*, Special report: Executive pay, April 19,1999). Executive salaries outstripped both company performance and increases in stock value, even during a time when virtually all stock values increased rapidly.

But what of this "average worker" we keep touting? What is the relationship between her labor and the profit that feeds this organizational frenzy? Any introduction to economics textbook will tell us that in order to generate a profit, workers must produce more value than they are paid in wages. At the same time, we are also told that, rather than exploiting workers, this transfer of surplus capital (profits) from workers to those who manage them represents the added value of managers' and executives' contributions to output. Besides, the argument continues, a large majority of all income generated by corporations goes to pay labor costs. According to the World Bank, US manufacturing wages in 1966 equaled 46% of the valued added in production. By 1990, that figure had fallen to 36%. And, while salaries increased in the 1990s, they scarcely kept up with profits.

The psychological and social effects of valuing management over labor are legion and have been hotly debated since the early days of this republic. Consider Abraham Lincoln's words: "Labor is prior to, and independent of, capital. Capital is only the fruit of labor, and could never have existed if labor had not first existed. Labor is the superior of capital, and deserves much the higher consideration." So, rather than catalog all the fallout from a system that rewards richly those at the top, but merely sustains those at the bottom, let us point out what may be its most chilling effect. A recent study of the distribution of wealth in each of the 50 states revealed that the gap between richest and poorest, rather than the average income in each state, was the best predictor of mortality (Kaplan, Pamuk, Lynch, Cohen & Balfour 1996).

Ameaning in the "New Economy"

We assume that our readers are, like most of the American population, so familiar with the surfeit of recent corporate scandals that additional retelling is unnecessary. While mere mention of the names "Enron," "Global Crossing," and "WorldCom" evokes some outrage, the overall social response to this systemic harm is muted by unconscious adaptation to domination. The spectacle of corporate executives acquiring great wealth at the expense of workers (and shareholders), and then escaping punishment for their illegal activities, confirms the sadistic and immoral underpinnings of culturally sanctioned rules for corporate (and government) behavior.

These corporate cases suggest that it is time to ponder our unspoken pledge of allegiance to an organizational ideology that relies on power and domination (the two key ingredients in morally cruel behavior) to sustain itself. The chapter should not be read as a suggestion that non-dominating forms of organization are the only solution, nor as an apology for left-wing economic ideology. Our critique here is intended, however, as a call to examine meaningfully the effects of organizational life on individual behavior, coupled with an argument that there are alternative systems that can and have been conceptualized. In like manner, history provides us with numerous examples of first perceiving, then addressing and ultimately changing what had been theretofore hidden oppression in social institutions. To the abolition of slavery and the women's movement, we can add child labor laws, workplace safety requirements, and the development of less coercive and toxic alternatives to organizing work.

Consciously choosing to organize our work life in a manner that creates opportunity without facilitating oppression remains an open option. The question, of course, is whether we have the courage to pursue it.

> [M]odels have to be appropriate to the time in which you are living, and our time has changed so fast that what was proper fifty years ago is not proper today. The virtues of the past are the vices of today. And many of what were thought to be the vices of the past are the necessities of today. The moral order has to catch up with the moral necessities of actual life in time, here and now" (Campbell 1988: 13).

Chapter Six

Nationalism: A Descent into Ameaning

with contributing authors Maria Czyzewska and Yasmin Lodi

> *Patriotism is the last refuge to which a scoundrel clings.*
> *Steal a little and they throw you in jail,*
> *steal a lot and they make you king.*
> —*Bob Dylan*

> *Definition of a Nation: "a group of people united by a mistaken view about the past and a hatred of their neighbors."*
> —*Ernest Renan*

It was a miserably cold, wet fall evening when the woman from India stepped into a bus in Bucharest, joining a few other passengers whose dour expressions did not invite any human connection. A young street kid hopped on, too. Whistling happily and wearing a beguiling smile, he stretched his hand out to the few riders. The glares he invoked did not deter him. He grabbed the steel bar in the center of the bus and swung around it, a private celebration that transformed the cold steel bar into an accommodating May pole. At the next stop two men entered. Their first act in the nearly empty coach was to lay claim to the bar, dislodge the kid, and aim a barrage of disparaging remarks at his back as he quietly withdrew from the contest. Catching the woman's disapproving eye, one of the young men responded with, "Dirty Gypsy," as if that sufficiently explained the group's behavior. They had effectively silenced the only happy sound in the bus.

Later, getting off the bus, the woman noticed a swastika drawn by a human finger in the condensation on the glass door. For a split second she was tempted to wipe it off, to deny the reality. The moment passed and with it her impulse to hide from it. Instead it endured, a symbolic representation of the quiet tragedy she left behind—indelibly imprinted in her mind.

From the vantage developed in this volume, what are we to make of this seemingly simple exchange? The boy was a free rider, so he had no business being on the bus; he was filthy and he probably carried all kinds of contagion; he was homeless and did not really have any place in particular to go. But the most telling artifact of this event drawn from everyday life comes down to one word: Gypsy.

Ameaning in Nationalism

The waves of violence that flow from nationalistic fervor seem perpetually on the rise. Few of us can watch the evening news without sensing at least some vestige of the ensuing undercurrents of violence— from Kosovo, Chechnya/ Dagestan, and East Timor to the Middle East and Israel or the United States and Iraq. Although we generally associate nationalism with civil wars and ethnic tensions, values defined by geography and ethnicity filter our perceptions of ways to live. By directing our attention to concerns particular to our national group, these values influence how we perceive and interact with those who belong to our national in-group—as opposed to those who do not belong.

The unfortunate reality is that distinctions between "nationalism" and "patriotism" are commonly collapsed in ordinary discourse. Both have come to reflect a kind of group narcissism wherein personal pride is enhanced simply by "belonging" to a particular group. At the outset, we can surmise that the toxicity of natio-centric perception occurs along the fault lines that distinguish in-group/out-group membership. Once we assign a person to a category (Gypsy), then we may alter the rules regarding how we should treat this particular individual.

There is no consensus among social theorists regarding the formal definition of nationalism. It is described variously as a belief, idea, ideal, identity, process, and political expression of the nation's aspirations (Barrington 1997). As difficult as the concept may be to pin down, we can identify five assumptions that are central to its manifestation: (1) loyalty to a particular nation; (2) confidence that national interest is superior to all other considerations; (3) worship of national characteristics; (4) conviction that national culture must be preserved at all cost; and (5) belief (often implicit) that nation-states represent the "natural" state of human organization and therefore life must be organized accordingly (Benn 1967: 442-443).

Walter Wink (1992) argues that this collage of assumptions unerringly defines what he refers to as "domination systems," that is, systems that rely on a hidden or disguised power base and that advance the goals of a particular group. When a system of domination becomes interwoven with a national identity, then personal identity and group identity are collapsed: Interpersonal relations and international relations can both be structured according to a pattern of domination. The result, according to Simone Weil, is that "Human history is simply the history of the servitude which makes men—oppressors and oppressed alike—the plaything of the instruments of domination they themselves have manufactured, and thus reduces living humanity to being the chattel of inanimate chattels" (Weil 1973: 69).

Both Weil and Wink understand that eventually the domination game transforms all players into the same profile, because "Everything that is subjected to the contact of force is defiled." For instance, in considering tit-for-tat nuclear proliferation—whether the historical cold war of superpowers or the more recent India versus Pakistan vintage—what do we find? According to Wink, we find two "domination systems" that are far more alike than either side is willing or able to see. "The irony is that successful defense against a power–maximizing aggressor requires a society to become more like the society that threatens it. Thus domination is a contaminant, a disease that, once introduced will inexorably spread throughout the system of societies." Once a contest for domination is put into play, "everyone is forced to become involved" (Wink 1992: 40-41).

The general principle ensuing from this analysis is that even when we "win" the domination game, we "lose." Here Wink is at his best, leading us to an insight that connects our concentric circles of ameaningful reasoning and justified cruelty to institutional pyramids of power:

> Those of us who now enjoy affluence and freedom as well as power are predisposed to believe that benign forces shape our destiny. But to the extent that our blessings are incidental by-products of our citizenship in nations that currently enjoy domination status over others, our well-being may be more a result of flagrant injustice than divine providence.
>
> The pain of living a life so alienated from what is natural and pleasurable exacts a psychic cost. . . . Most of us, winners and losers alike, are profoundly unable to grasp the severity of our loss. Numbness in turn produces amnesia about what a fully human life would be like, and even a fear of remembering. We internalize the ethic of productivity, the constraints of patriarchy, the imperative of success, the drivenness of modern life, the obligations of machismo, the laws that prevent our achieving for ourselves what the powerful achieve at our expense. We become complicit.

And so we leave unopposed the world that injures us, restructuring ourselves to appease the Powers we depend upon. To
achieve peace with the world, we declare war upon ourselves
(Wink 1992: 42-43).

For Wink (1992: 95-96), the implicit (ameaningful) assumptions
that underpin nationalism are these:

- Rulers (whether elected or not) "should be rewarded by
  extra privileges and greater wealth of all kinds."

- "Those who have military strength, who control the most
  advanced technology, the greatest wealth, or the largest
  markets, are the ones who will and should survive."

- "Property is sacred, and property ownership an absolute
  right."

- "Great size is proof of. . . power and value."

- "There is no higher value or being than the state. If there
  is a God, God is the protector and patron of the state."

- "God, if there is one, is not revealed to all, but only to
  select. . . nations and their rulers and priesthood."

Connecting these assumptions in step-wise fashion is probably
not the most effective way to convey their influence. Instead, it is perhaps
best to think of the set of assumptions as a collage, one that simultaneously
accomplishes three outcomes. First, the ascendancy of the collective over
the individual is established. Second, the individual not only accepts the
relegation, but enthusiastically embraces it (with patriotic fervor). And
third, the individual, having subordinated self-direction to nationalistic
agenda, will now perceive reality from that vantage point.

Simone Weil remarked that "what is generally named egoism is
not love of self, it is a defect of perspective" (in Frost & Bell-Metereau
1998: 39). Illustrating the role that nationalism contributes to a defect
of perception, she observed that the "massacre of one hundred thousand
Chinese hardly alters the order of the world as [non-Chinese persons]

perceive it, but if instead a fellow worker has a slight rise in pay which they have not, the order of the world is turned upside down!. . . [They] only apply the idea of legitimate order to the immediate neighborhood of their hearts" (1998: 39).

We may say, then, that nationalistic fervor functions as a psychological boundary, one that demarcates the neighborhood of our hearts. The further a person or persons lie beyond that boundary— psychologically, if not geographically—the more our attention is attuned to justification and the less it is attuned to harm.

Nationalism and the Ambiguity of Patriotism

Patriotism lies at the conceptual periphery of nationalism. The question remains whether the two concepts can be reliably differentiated, in kind if not in cause. Charles Taylor insists that "the democratic state needs a healthy degree of what used to be called 'patriotism,' a strong sense of identification with the polity, and a willingness to give of oneself for its sake" (McKim & McMahan 1997: 40). In its original meaning, Taylor maintains, patriotism or the love of one's fatherland meant loving its laws. He sees "no reference to a prepolitical identity." Similarly, Alter contends that "Unlike nationalism, patriotism has virtually never had the effect of an aggressive political force" (1989: 6). Further, he notes that patriotism has only recently—that is, since the nineteenth century—come to mean allegiance to the nation and nation-state.

While these distinctions are useful in understanding the intellectual history of patriotism, they are not so clear in practice. Where, for instance, does tribal or community spirit end and patriotism or nationalism begin? Nathanson argues that "many people who are patriotic do not think of themselves as nationalists, but patriotism is simply another name for nationalism. As such, it inspires in people a partiality or special concern for their own nation and motivates its adherents to promote their own nation's well-being" (McKim & McMahan 1997: 178). Patriotism implicitly demands that because we love our country and the principles upon which it is established, we should attempt to impose our principles abroad. What can we say about the hubris that allows us to conclude that we know what is best for the world as a whole and thus that we hold a moral obligation to determine the fate of other nations?

Belief in the superiority of a particular national identity may be inherently ameaningful. To arrive at such an *a priori* position requires willful ignorance of the complex geopolitical and cultural contexts that define (and have always defined) life on earth. To ignore the ambiguities of complex situations and, instead, force a simplistic nationalist agenda onto a global frame represents a failure of attention and a failure of reason. Where this ameaningful reasoning is coupled with the use of force, the probability of moral cruelty is high. Indeed, by the time we reach such a point, the inherent logic of power and domination replace the potential of human thought and measured choice. As Wink puts it, "The Domination System has constrained the profound transformations in the evolution of human civilization in such a manner that human destiny is no longer governed by free human choice. 'No one is free to choose peace, but anyone can impose upon all the necessity for power'" (Wink 1992: 41).

In other words, we now appear destined to follow in the footsteps of the Light Brigade, an event of the Crimean War (1853-1856), as poignantly portrayed by Alfred Lord Tennyson:

> 'Forward, the Light Brigade!'
> Was there a man dismay'd?
> Not tho' the soldier knew
> Some one had blunder'd.
> Theirs not to make reply,
> Theirs not to reason why,
> Theirs but to do and die.
> Into the valley of Death
>
> Rode the six hundred.

As we have cautioned, however, moral cruelty may take a multitude of forms. Although the more common ameaningful guise seems to be the automatic use of force to further a national agenda, the more subtle case involves situations where ameaningful moral structures lead us *not* to intervene in a situation where harm is occurring. Nobel Peace Laureate Elie Wiesel, speaking of his experience in Nazi concentration camps, reported that the suffering caused by perceiving a world that seemed unwilling to intervene was more intense than the physical suffering within the camps. The manuscript of his first book, published as *Night*, had originally been titled *And the World Was Silent*.

Unfortunately, the ambiguity does not end here. At the fiscal periphery of nationalism lies another common justification for using force against other nations—national economic interest. To begin, one would think that the traffic of arms from North Korea and China to Libya and Iran and Syria illustrate this tendency—that nation-states "will consort with any civilization, however alien, as long as the price is right and the goods are ready" (Huntington 1993: 6). Conversely, individuals justify their dislike of immigrants on economic grounds: Cheap immigrant labor destroys the financial fabric of the nation. The more widespread the sentiment, the greater the likelihood of assaults against members of immigrant communities. Or, to return to the context within which the Trang Bang bombing occurred, we can paraphrase one "negative reading" of the war in Vietnam War as a story of drafting predominantly black, brown and poor white men to go and kill yellow men in order to defend a land taken by force from red men for the sake of wealthy white men. Other perspectives on the Vietnam conflict are possible, of course, and to perceive such a complex event in simple, one-dimensional terms is ameaningful in itself. The point of alternative renderings (to those rendered in nationalistic terms) is this: To dismiss outright any consideration of the roles that nationalism and economic interest in general, and socioeconomic status and ethnicity in particular, might have played in prior military excursions is to take refuge in collective justification.

At the gendered periphery of nationalism, we find horrendous acts of justified cruelty against women. The Taliban's form of nationalism provided an extreme example. Even prior to 9-11, the suicide rate among women in Afghanistan was the highest in the world. A generation of educated, professional, and modern women were literally destroyed in the name of religiously-defined nationalism. Similarly, women in several countries of North Africa undergo genital mutilation in the name of culture and tradition, an act that their nation-states protect as a cultural right. In India, bride-burning and the practice of *Sati* have been criminalized for years, and yet one still hears of their occurrence.

And at the sociocultural periphery of nationalism we find a deep distress and distrust that circumvents any impulse toward unity in one's homeland. In short, the lines of social demarcation do not always coincide with the physical boundaries of the nation-state. Often the boundaries are drawn between communities occupying the same space, between individuals belonging to the same ethnic group, and even between members of the same family. Children of international marriages, for example, often feel the tug of two different national loyalties.

In such sub-groups we find a structure of exclusion similar to that of full-blown nationalism: loyalty to a collective that is perceived as "more worthy" than other collectives, that must be preserved at all costs, and hence one that is due allegiance from its constituents. Even at the micro-level, affiliation with a collective often promotes a heightened sense of self-worth, a sense of security and belonging, and a crystallized frame of identity. Who could argue against such desirable outcomes?

A Descent into Ameaning

Following our delineation of ameaningful reasoning and justified cruelty thus far, our response to the question of "desirable outcomes" is that we can argue for those outcomes, but not without consideration of cost. Psychologists ourselves, we acknowledge and appreciate the value of personal worth, belongingness, security, and identity. When those outcomes are procured at the expense of others, however, we can and do challenge what is gained with the issue of what is lost—and by whom.

Further, as we dig deeper into the anatomy of cruelty, we will suggest that such surface outcomes not only harm others, but may imperceptibly sow seeds of self-destructiveness as well.

The initial step toward ameaning occurs when we mindlessly internalize the notion of loyalty; we do not simply pledge allegiance, we pledge blind allegiance. The ubiquity of this tendency is concretely manifest by automobile bumper stickers, especially in the United States, where the automobile is sacrosanct. During the Vietnam conflict, and the strident protests against that war, literally thousands of Americans posted this message for all to see: "America: Love it or Leave it." "My country: Right or Wrong."

Lest we think the mindset—and the urge to advertise it—is simply historical artifact, we need only fast forward to post 9-11 America. The same shopworn slogans have re-emerged, together with a need to adorn one's vehicle with the American flag (or several of them). Elected officials in Washington D.C. have publicly warned other officials who disagree with national policy (e.g., the "war on terrorism") to "keep their mouths shut." "Profiling," and active distrust of and aggression toward "others," has reached new heights. Indeed, we may be living in an epoch where ameaningful reasoning and justified harm have attained record levels.

In suggesting that current national climate reflects tell-tale signs of ameaningfulness, we do not suggest that the proper cause of action to events that precipitated the change is obvious and clear. As we referenced above, Nobel Peace Laureate Elie Wiesel cautions us that lack of intervention can also constitute ameaningful morality: We jump to "good reasons" not to intervene and look the other way, and harm continues unabated. Any suggestion, then, that we could render clearly the events of 9-11 and all events subsequent to that attack, in one chapter of one book no less, would itself constitute ameaningful reasoning.

We can, however, identify broad themes that accompanied the attack, and identify the direction of those actions and reactions along a meaning/ameaning continuum. From our vantage point, we argue that a "Top 5" hallmarks of ameaningful reasoning recently employed in the service of nationalism included:

- An immediate, automatic response to retaliate against "them," especially when the "them" was both ill-defined and generalized beyond the realm of actual perpetrators.

- An inability to perceive contradictions between one's internalized moral codes (e.g., "love thine enemies") and the active pursuit of actions designed to kill others.

- An inability to consider whether initiating specific courses of retaliation would actually lessen a cycle of hatred and increase collective security, versus increase a cycle of hatred and increase the likelihood of repeated attacks.

- An inability to question why a new "sworn enemy" (e.g., Osama bin Laden) was originally an ally of, and trained and militarily-equipped by, the United States.

- An immediate, automatic, and venomous response against persons who dared to question the national response to the original attack.

In using violence and aggression as a political tool, we see a parallel structure to parents who hit their children in order to teach them not to hit. And where we see innocent persons killed in the 9-11 attack as "victims," we hear our patriotic leaders dismiss the loss of innocent lives overseas as "collateral damage"—with little soul-searching on the part of Americans. As we indicated in Chapter 1, one hallmark of ameaningful reasoning involves judging the actions of others negatively, yet judging those same actions when performed by one's own reference group as "justified," or even positive. As we defend our forceful response in the name of "freedom and democracy," we simultaneously and systematically attempt to silence all persons with whom we disagree: "Keep your mouths shut." "Love it or leave it."

How difficult is it, really, to see the threads of ameaning inherent in such a nationalistic tapestry?

Chapter Seven

Religion: Meaning and Ameaning in Narrative

with contributing author Stan Friedman

Do justice, love mercy and be holy unto your God.

Those who make you believe absurdities can make you commit atrocities.

—*Voltaire*

By now, you are no doubt familiar with the theme and structure of our book. Chapter by chapter, we offer an example of a seemingly "justified" scenario, and then seek to peel away the layers of the story—searching for the clandestine element of harm. As we stated at the outset, it is our belief that such everyday incidents of moral harmfulness contribute to a climate within which more pronounced cruelty occurs. So it is with religion. For this chapter, a gruesome description of the torturing of Jews during the Spanish Inquisition or Crusades, a report of some recent violence from the Hindu-Moslem conflict in India, or a compelling description of the sadistic treatment of women under the Taliban would certainly capture attention. More subtle, perhaps, would be a story of children forced to perform noxious tasks because "idle hands are the devil's tools," or parents who hit children out of a fear that "to spare the rod spoils the child," or the "benign" subordination of women by mainstream religious denominations because "God has willed it so."

As upsetting as examples of justified cruelty from prior chapters may be, there is something perhaps even more disturbing about the use of religion to sanctify violence and harm. Though censorship, for example, is sufficiently troublesome when justified by political reasons, it seems even worse when done in the name of God and Truth. Take the case of Salman Rushdie. Here we saw a person condemned to death for writing a book, and literally millions of people would have considered killing him a holy deed. Our response to religious varieties of sadism is heightened because religion not only appeals to human power, but purports to put us in concert with a higher power. Ultimately religion claims to be about sacred, absolute standards of right and wrong, of what is moral and immoral—attributed to a divine reality. When we look at justified cruelty in the religious sphere, therefore, we may expect to encounter covert harm in its most ritualized form.

It is a Sunday morning in 1962, in Alpine, Texas, a small West Texas town far removed from such political realities as a Cuban missile crisis. A young boy, only nine-years-old, is attending a Sunday school class at the First (Southern) Baptist Church. The choice of attendance was not originally his, but a decision imposed by parents. On this day, the teacher has homed in on the fact that every child in this class has been "saved" except for this one boy. Therefore, the teacher and the other children are encouraging the boy to make that decision, to choose to be saved. They carefully explain that, should he die before making the decision, he would go to hell, where he would burn in flames forever. This explanation, of course, is couched in a narrative of love and caring for the boy and his destiny.

Whether possessed of a stubborn temperament or a vivid imagination, this young boy naively asks: "But what if I had been born in another country, and never even heard the name of Jesus; would I still go to hell?" Yes, he was told, there was "one way" to escape hell, and one way only. There really were only two types of people in the world, he learned: the saved and the unsaved. Even many of those who called themselves "Christians" were in reality unsaved. This situation, the boy was reassured, was all part of "God's plan."

That same day, during the "invitational hymn" that concludes each Southern Baptist service, this young boy walked down the aisle and was asked by the preacher: "Do you accept Jesus Christ as your personal savior?" Not understanding the question, the young boy replied simply that he wanted to be baptized; he wanted to be saved. The following Sunday night, during an evening worship service, this young boy was baptized. In the eyes of his parents, his teachers, the Baptist businessmen of Alpine, and a multitude of his fellow religious Americans, he was now "saved."

In this co-author's true story (CJF), the bringing together of concentric circles in a religious moment of truth, we find a hallmark of religion: It permeates many, if not all, other facets of individual and social existence. For believers and non-believers alike, religion is present in many aspects of our lives, even without our knowing it. Religion provides one of the bases for the state's interest in marriage, justifies tax credits for contributions to our churches, and garners tax exemptions for real estate valued in the billions of dollars. It is found in our homes, where it is sometimes used to cement loving family relations and sometimes used to justify wife abuse and child abuse. It guides many persons who are experiencing grief and provides rituals for dealing with the deaths of those we love. Religious beliefs may influence whom we choose to marry, and the way in which we formalize that marriage; how we structure our family; what we do with our money; and with whom we should, or should not, have sex—and how and when we "should" do so. We may also incorporate religious belief into our perceptions of ourselves, as the core of our identity; how we do so may influence our sense of personal worth. Indeed, the influence of religion in our lives is almost endless, whether or not we consciously adhere to an organized religious system.

Most importantly, religious beliefs (or an explicit rejection thereof) constitute a primary source for our attributions, a basis from which we attempt to comprehend why things happen as the days of our lives unfold. In other words, as persons try to understand events that seem inexplicable from the vantage point of everyday reality, they willingly shift to a perspective that purports to make sense of non-sense, that provides comfort or certainty in the face of uncertainty and indeterminism. The greater the ambiguity in what we see, the greater may be the pull for a system of symbols that provides structure and meaning to the amorphous mass we call reality.

Religious as Narrative Symbol System

By religion, we mean a group of at least somewhat unified practices and beliefs related to approaching, delineating, producing or understanding what may be considered divine, sacred (literally, "set apart") or transcendent. Religious beliefs and rituals are held in common by a group of people, and these beliefs often comprise the most powerful, unifying force of that group. While our definition of a religious system would include Judaism, Christianity, Islam and other mainline Western religions, as well as many Eastern belief systems, it might also include non-mainstream systems of meaning as well, including those that get branded as "cults." Religion may offer a vision of what the world should be like, as well as dictates regarding how we should act so as to transform the world to what it should be. Religious beliefs may be concerned with how to keep God or the higher powers happy, and how to continue to earn or receive divine blessings. Religion is also a means of trying to keep or bring the world back into balance, particularly after a loss or traumatic event.

A key criterion of religion is that a group of persons share a common set of symbols, embedded in story, that binds them together as a group and that is perceived as connecting them to reality—natural or supra-natural. By story, or myth, we refer to the presence of a symbol system, a narrative, without presuming to judge the veracity of its content.

The fact that we seek meaning through stories appears to be part of the human condition. People tend to embrace stories to explain what they do not understand. The bigger the mystery, the greater the ambiguity, then the bigger and more powerful the story must be to explain it. The stories that religions tell are complex, and the characters involved tend to be larger than life. They reflect on or appeal to morality, that is to some larger power that defines what is right and wrong, that provides a guide to actions as well as to thoughts. And they often attempt to help us see the moral blueprint that defines a unified whole, that is, that reflects God's or a higher power's structural plan.

These stories are so important and so pervasive that they might be called a unifying myth. The narrative promotes identification, connection, and solidarity, giving the group a sense of power and efficacy. In so doing, the stories may provide structure, meaning, and purpose for their adherents, while masking a program of harm toward non-adherents. Where fear and guilt are used to convey and enhance the intensity of the message, there may be pronounced toxicity involved, even for adherents to the myth.

Consider a recurring Halloween tale, for example. Each year Trinity Church, an Assembly of God church in Cedar Hill, Texas, sets up an "alternative" haunted house dubbed "Hell House." In October 1999, the house included a reenactment of the Columbine school attack. When queried by a reporter about the wisdom of such a display, religious leaders involved offered a number of justifications. Tim Ferguson, youth pastor of that Assembly of God church, hoped that "maybe I can make one person think not to do it." Another pastor, Dave McPherson, said that this portrayal "hit too close to home. . . even though it's not my style, I can see that it can serve a purpose. . . . There will be kids who will come to that who will never go to church, and it may be their only exposure to the church." Even Cassandra Chance, a friend of a Columbine shooting victim, said: "My gut reaction was repulsiveness. . . But I think if the message is getting out, that's the point of it." As of this writing (Halloween, 2002), additional "scare them to goodness" haunted houses are cropping up elsewhere in the state.

While we agree that there is a message here, once again we disagree with the rendering of that message. In the first place, allowing churches to offer such a tableau of terror immediately raises a number of questions about narrative and about power. Hell House is an imaginative creation of persons in charge of the church; we have a domination system at work. And once again the end is seen as justifying the means: witnessing the spectacle of death is "for our own good" and "will prevent us from going and doing likewise." According to the social psychological research literature, however, persons witnessing degradation are far more likely to become desensitized to violence, that is, to come to see it as normal, than they are to learn some prosocial message. Further, we see again

Moral Cruelty

the extrinsic grammar of compliance at work. Rather than viewing morality as the mindful internalization of such attributes as compassion, empathy, and honesty in our dealings with others—and the ability to apply meaningfully such abstract principles to concrete life events—morality is perceived through the lens of fear and repulsion. Is there, in fact, any credible evidence that fearful or traumatized persons somehow seek a more compassionate, charitable path in life? Or that such persons more readily engage in meaningful moral reasoning?

A meaningful religious coda teaches us not only to fear others, particularly those who do not share our story, but also to fear our own selves—to be afraid of what we think and feel, to be afraid of being human. Fearfulness of self is often supported by a dogma of evil, a narrative shred that teaches us that we are evil at heart—in need of "saving." When this motif of innate evil is coupled to a belief in some external source of evil, we are led to dissociate part of ourselves from ourselves. "The devil made me do it" is a coda of dissociation, a splitting of self that prohibits integration of personality. And it is precisely that "splitting apart" that most enables us to engage in violence, in cruelty. While one part of me commits the harm, another part of me focuses on a different part of self—the part that "believes the right story," that is moral.

One derivation of the word "devil" connects the term to the Greek *dia bollein*, to separate or break asunder (Csikszentmihalyi 1997: 147). Thus, to fail at the task of integration is to be diabolical. The greater the disparity within ourselves, the greater our capacity to do harm, and to remain blind to the harm we inflict. Claims to unifying experience notwithstanding, a meaningful threads inherent in some religious tapestries may promote a dis-integration of self.

By serving as a barrier to self-development and to a capacity for positive social relatedness, toxic religiosity sows seeds of destructiveness along two paths. First, even where persons come to reject the myth and its motivational structure of fear and guilt, they may not yet know with what story to replace it—how to go about creating their own story or choosing to share a more positive narrative. Case studies of persons who depart rigid, rulebound religion, only to suffer a sort of "psychic bleeding"—a numbed existence as if drifting in a vacuum—abound.

Secondly, where persons are unable to move beyond the story, they are more likely to become the blindly obedient, fanatical types who can seamlessly harm others in the service of their myth. As we complete final editing of this book, the most recent public example is Eric Rudolph. Rudolph's acts of moral cruelty apparently include the bombings of a gay nightclub, the bombings of at least two abortion clinics, and a bombing of the 1996 Atlanta Olympics. Labeling Rudolph a "Christian terrorist," columnist Leonard Pitts correctly nails down how this story is likely to play: Millions of Christians who used the case of Osama bin Laden to denounce Islam *in toto* will now cry "foul" when being judged as a community that includes Rudolph.

> The story is almost certainly apocryphal, but here it is for what it's worth. Soon after the Sept. 11 terrorist attacks, Muhammad Ali was supposedly visiting Ground Zero when someone asked a barbed question: How did Ali, the most famous Muslim in the world who is not a terrorist, feel about sharing his religion with Osama bin Laden? The champ shot back, 'How does it feel to share yours with Hitler?'

> [The story]. . . is probably not true, but it ought to be. It's valuable for what is says about our tendency to demonize the unfamiliar and overlook the obvious. . . . [Rudolph] is indeed thought to have been motivated by Christianity. . . .

> So does that make him a Christian terrorist? And if not, why? What is the substantive difference between him and all the "Muslim terrorists" who plant bombs out of their supposed devotion to Islam? (*Austin American-Statesman* June 9: 2003)

The role of narrative does not end with the story of evil. Through the telling of stories, religion becomes a way of trying to understand the otherwise unexplainable mysteries of life: birth, luck, happiness, death, and one's sense of place in the world and the universe. We use the stories to help us decide what causes what, as well as to decide what we should do in situations for which we do not yet have an answer.

For example, should we kill a person who kills someone else? It is possible to use the "eye for an eye" text from the Tanach to support capital punishment, but among western nations, only the United States seems to interpret the narrative in this way. Or, how do we understand differences in wealth among people? As discussed in a previous chapter, a defining myth of capitalism is that the accumulation of capital is not only good for business, but that it is also a defining good for individuals. The myth provides a loftier, more noble motive for accumulating wealth than simple greed: It is the best and most efficient way to distribute goods and services to people in need. Capitalism can be used to justify everything from the abuse of migrant and sweat shop garment workers to the inequitable distribution of wealth. By connecting one's religion to one's nation and its organizations, the camouflage may be made even more complete. As God's chosen people, why shouldn't we enjoy the lion's share of the world's resources?

The stamping of "In God we Trust" on our currency is not coincidental, nor perhaps is this most telling of outcomes: The five-hundred (500) wealthiest individuals in the world (almost all of whom are American) now control more resources than the three-billion (3,000,000,000) poorest people on the planet (Loeb 1999: 3).

How is it that systems of meaning that prod us to "love others" and to "do unto others as you would have them do to you" comfortably co-exist with and even contribute to such outcomes as crusades, pogroms, civil wars, retaliatory strikes, and gross disparities in wealth? And how is it possible to use religion even to justify the killing of persons who reside under the same umbrella of faith, such as the assassination of Rabin by fellow Jews or the tit-for-tat slaughter of Protestants and Catholics in Northern Ireland?

Before using such examples to justify the challenging of religion *per se* and *in toto*—an uncritical and ameaningful tack to take—we need to juxtapose examples at the other end of the continuum. In the first week of November 1999, the brutal murderer of a gay student was convicted of murder in the second degree. We can point out that years of religious intolerance have contributed to the culture of hatred against homosexuals. Shortly after apologizing for decades of institutionalized racism, for instance, the Southern Baptists officially turned to a systematic persecution of homosexuals by calling for a boycott of Disney, a company that had adopted non-discriminatory policies regarding sexual orientation. However, there is more to the story.

The father of the murdered student, experiencing not only the anguish inherent in the loss of his son, but also the hurt accompanying the knowledge of the grim cruelty of the murder, got his chance to address the jury during the sentencing phase of the trial. Rather than arguing for the death penalty, as do many family members of murder victims, the father of Matthew Shepherd argued against it, citing his religious belief. While acknowledging that part of him wanted the murderer to die for what he had done, he continued to engage in meaningful moral reasoning—including activation of moral themes structured by forgiveness and reconciliation.

And the outcome? His mindful moral reasoning led him to intervene on the behalf of the murderer of his own son.

During the same time interval as the resolution of Matthew Shepherd's murder, another story broke, this one reporting on a businessman who had taken his company public for a large sum of money. Unlike others, however, this businessman did not retain the profits solely for himself. To the contrary, he declared that it was the 550+ employees who had produced the wealth, and he then proceeded to distribute over one-hundred million dollars among them equally.

Or consider another example. Nearly three decades later, that boy from Alpine, Texas, finds himself in the depths of Romanian orphanages—struggling to combat the abysmal harm inflicted daily on infants and children. As he looks around for allies in this struggle, who did he find standing there at his side? None other than religious emissaries from across the theological spectrum (Southern Baptist, Catholic, Mormon, and more). And who did he *not* see there? Representatives from professional associations with which he is affiliated, including scientific societies, psychological associations, and associations of university professors. Indeed, a professor from Drury University (affiliated with the Disciples of Christ and the United Church of Christ) responded during a conference presentation that "those children are no concern of ours," this during a discussion on "globalization and ethics." It appears that, for many, he is all too correct: the plight of Romanian orphans, or of children living in abject conditions in numerous world locales, remains barely a blip on the professional associations' and university circuit radar screens.

In spite of widely divergent, internalized narrative systems, we find individuals that have noticed Romanian orphans, attended to their plight as a moral situation, and intervened actively on their behalf. Thus, it is not any particular, singular belief that can "explain" these perceptions and interventions. Indeed, after heartfelt dialogue with persons of divergent stories, we discovered a common turning point: one look at these innocents was all it took to perceive the harm (remember Plummer and the photograph). No prefabricated justification successfully cloaked that harm, once perceived, regardless of narrative. When all is said and done, this common ability to see the harm and then act to remedy the harm conveys an important element in our attempt to articulate a *perceptual* theory of morality.

It seems we are faced, yet again, with paradox, with contradiction. The power of myth, especially the religious vintage, seems able to activate both the highest and the lowest within human beings. Even the *same* myth, like that narrative spun around the figure of Jesus, can be used to justify the hating of homosexuals (see, for example, the Westboro Baptist Church website, http://www.godhatesfags.com/) and, simultaneously, it can be used to motivate forgiveness of those persons who are engaging in precisely that form of moral cruelty.

Examining the importance of myth, the basis of its power, might help us understand this inherent contradiction. Because they are the stories we tell in order to understand or explain great mysteries, religious stories are able to snare the most central dimensions of human existence. Myths are less statements that can be adjudged true or false empirically than they are stories that meet us where we are in life—stories that we can understand and use. In fact, religion is often *the* myth of personal meaning, because within many of its stories one finds answers to virtually every aspect of existence. The language of myth *is* its power.

Myth: The Language of Faith

Language, the carrier of story, is in some ways the ultimate social arbitrator. We use language to watch and keep track of ourselves and others. Merlin Donald (1991) suggests that the most elevated use of language in tribal society is what he calls "mythic invention," that is, constructed models of the human universe. Essentially all cultures, no matter how "primitive" or unchanging, hold myths about how the world was created, why we are born and why we die. Other stories encapsulate the shared ideas and history of the tribe (1999: 213-214). In many such societies the myths are so important and powerful that they are publicly mentioned only rarely, and often only by the initiated—at the appointed time. In contemporary societies, however, it is more common for us all to be initiates and to talk about our myths at any time.

But myth also involves how we integrate (or fail to integrate) our personal episodes into the larger stories using special symbols. For example, we can feel blessed by God or say that we have good Karma, as opposed to just being lucky. Our story essentially gives shape to, embodies, our experience. It helps us combine many apparently unrelated episodes of our lives into something coherent: a tapestry of meaning woven from those frightening and apparently meaningless threads of life. "Myth is the inevitable outcome of narrative skill and is the supreme organizing principle" (Donald 1991: 258).

With myth we can communicate not only facts, but feelings and values—often without our being explicitly aware of it. For example, a friend who knows that a colleague of ours is Jewish said to him, with no sense of irony or intended cruelty, that a health problem he was having was "his cross to bear." Although the friend may not consciously be aware of all layers of meanings of the Jesus myth (bearing the cross), it nonetheless permeates her Christian culture and shapes her experience. This tacit dimension of experience can make for difficulties when myths collide, for then we need face the question, "Which myth should prevail?"

Herein lies another dimension to the structure of ameaningful reasoning and justified cruelty: a tendency to foist one's own myths and meanings onto others, by failing to perceive the diversity of myths through which human beings find meaning. A school board in Central Texas, for example, is currently appealing to the Supreme Court for the right to petition the Supreme Being prior to their high school football games. They are couching this appeal in the language of "freedom of religion." A simple probe below the surface indicates a quite different reality. In the first place, any individual attending that event can at any moment choose to bow his or her head and pray. So what these Christians are really asking for is the right to force every single individual attending their games to listen to the public broadcast of a Christian prayer. In the second place, were the issue truly freedom of religion, then presumably any person, of any faith, should also be allowed to broadcast a prayer —to Adonai, Allah, the Tao, or whomever.

This episode unveils one of the most characteristic (but tacit) assumptions inherent not in religion or myth-making *per se*, but embedded in how many people learn to "hold," to process (mindlessly) their narrative belief: The assumption that if there is a God, He (assuming gender) has revealed himself to one group of individuals only. A corollary is that *our* narrative myths are true, while all other renditions are false. The world is divided into the ubiquitous two groups, "us" and "them," and we begin indoctrinating children into this division early in life—as our young boy of Alpine, Texas, experienced early on.

An insightful text that examines such toxic assumptions carefully was published recently (2002) by Charles Kimball, Professor and Chair of the Department of Religion at Wake Forest University—and ordained Baptist Minister. In his book, *When Religion Becomes Evil,* Kimball identifies specific characteristics of a move toward toxic religion, what we would identify as ameaningful religious reasoning.

The characteristic most germane to this chapter is that of staking out one's religious narrative as the absolute truth and the *only* absolute truth. "Authentic religious truth claims are never as inflexible and exclusive as zealous adherents insist. Corrupt religious truth claims always lack the liberating awareness that humans are limited as they search for and articulate religious truth" (Kimball 2002: 41). In what constitutes a precise confirmation of a key facet of ameaningful reasoning, Kimball argues that "people armed with absolute truth claims are closely linked to . . . various *justifications for acts otherwise understood to be unacceptable*" (2002: 44; italics added). As our theory of ameaningful reasoning suggests, even where content of the myths differs radically, the attempt to justify harm may play itself out in uncannily similar fashion:

> Osama bin Laden and Jerry Falwell seemed to agree on [the idea that God actively participated in the events of September 11]: bin Laden interpreted the destruction of the towers and the crash into the Pentagon as a sign of God's support for

> his struggle against evil; Falwell suggested these horrifying
> events were God's way of telling us of his displeasure with
> abortionists, pagans, feminists, the ACLU, People for the
> American Way, and gays and lesbians (Kimball 2002: 48).

Yet again, we encounter the chameleon nature of ameaning.

As Kimball subsequently argues, "clear thinking and honesty about one's sacred texts are not easy. Most people are not encouraged to ask critical questions within their own tradition. . . . My experience teaching intelligent undergraduates. . . reinforces the view that most Christians don't grow up learning to ask. . . basic questions about their own sacred texts" (2002: 59). And as W.K. Clifford noted, in the moral sphere of life it is the suppression of doubts and suspicions about the universality of one's beliefs, rather than the beliefs themselves, that creates immoral and cruel behavior (in Swinburne 1981).

Kimball relies on a work by Robert Alter, *The Art of Biblical Narrative*, wherein Alter echoes a central theme of meaningful thinking. Rather than understanding narrative as a process of mindless transmission from one generation to the next, Alter speaks (from within the Jewish tradition) of a need to seek actively, wrestle meaningfully, and re-define continually one's religious narrative:

> Indeed, an essential aim of the innovative techniques of
> fiction worked out by the ancient Hebrew writers was to
> produce a certain indeterminacy of meaning, especially
> in regard to motive, moral character, and psychology. . . .
> Meaning, perhaps for the first time in narrative literature, was
> conceived as a process, requiring continual revision—both
> in the ordinary sense and in the etymological sense of
> seeing–again—continual suspension of judgment, weighing
> of multiple possibilities, brooding over gaps in information
> provided (Alter 1981: 12).

Tempting as it may be to share our visions (particularly those of absolute truth vintage) only with those who already agree with us, that very impulse may be both counterproductive and destructive. As

M. Scott Peck puts it, "The great enemy of community is exclusivity. Groups that exclude others because they are poor or doubters or divorced or sinners or of some different race or nationality are not communities; they are cliques—actually defensive bastions against community." True communities are "always reaching to extend themselves" (in Loeb 1999: 215)

The problem, however, is this: Commonality comprises an essential thread of identity—both personal identity and community identity. A need to identify and align with others may not only be healthy, but essential to well-being. Social psychology research suggests that human beings are highly motivated to feel positively about themselves (Sedikides 1993). One method for doing this is to identify with groups and to garner some additional sense of self-definition from those affiliations (Deaux, Reid, Mizrahi & Cotting 1999). In an essay on hatred, Abraham Kaplan (1992) expressed this point even more forcefully:

> There is no reason why groups of shared identity should not establish their own communities, provided that there are no ghetto walls, whether their gates are locked from within or without, to preclude the acceptance of differences. To denounce as clannishness the warmth of feeling evoked by shared language, customs, and outlook is not to defend and cherish human values but to undermine them. The person who finds it equally easy to be friendly with everyone is no friend of mine. True, he might deserve veneration as a saint; it is more likely that he is controlling, uncaring, and superficial in his relationships (1992: 28).

The path to meaning, it seems, is something of a dialectical one. An inherent tension exists between the pull of identity and the push of exclusivity, as well as between a need to tolerate differences and uncertainty and an apparently strong propensity to want, need and demand certainty—absolute truth.

An ecumenical minister from Sri Lanka, Wesley Ariarajah, suggests a meaningful way to navigate these tensions. The point, says Ariarajah, is to remember that statements of faith, religious narratives, "derive their meaning in the context of faith and have no meaning outside the community of faith" (1985: 23). The key here is the notion of *relatedness*: What is absolute for me and my community need not be (indeed, by definition perhaps, cannot be) absolute for those outside myself or outside my community. Ariarajah then illustrates this principle concretely, simply, meaningfully:

> When my daughter tells me I'm the best daddy in the world, and there can be no other father like me, she is speaking the truth, for this comes out of her experience. She is honest about it; she knows no other person in the role of her father. But of course it is not true in another sense. For one thing, I myself know friends who, I think, are better fathers that I am. Even more importantly, one should be aware that in the next house there is another little girl who also thinks her daddy is the best father in the world. And she too is right. In fact at the level of the way the two children relate to their two fathers, no one can comprehend the truth content of the statements of the two girls. For here we are not dealing with the absolute truths, but with the language of faith and love. . . .
>
> The language of the Bible is also the language of faith.
>
> . . . The problem begins when we take these confessions in the language of faith and love and turn them into absolute truths. It becomes much more serious when we turn them into truths on the basis of which we begin to measure the truth or otherwise of other faith claims. My daughter cannot say to her little friend in the next house that there is no way she can have the best father, for the best one is right there in her house. If she does, we'll have to dismiss it as child-talk! (Ariarajah 1985: 25-26)

Now imagine a neighborhood of little girls or little boys who not only begin arguing over who's daddy is "really" the best, but begin killing each other over the question. As ridiculous as such a scenario may sound, it actually understates the reality of how competing truth claims have been enacted once we substitute "god" for "daddy."

Given the stakes, religious narratives literally are a matter of life versus death, or perhaps, infinite afterlife versus nothingness. To deal with the uncertainty and the underlying ambiguity it becomes all too easy, psychologically, to convert a need for certainty into a representation of certainty. Having done so, however, every system of meaning, every competing narrative that deviates from my own challenges the legitimacy of this "Truth." From this vantage, the death of my myth would mean the death of my very identity, now and forever; therefore, I am as likely to respond to an assault on my myth as forcefully (or more so) than an assault on my life.

When individuals or groups react in defense of core myths, attention is focused on the *rationale*—preserving the system of meaning —*not on any harm* that the response might impart. With attention to moral justification high, emotional arousal high, and attention to *what* is being done in the moment of defensive response low, the formula for moral cruelty is entirely in place. Once we grasp fully this structure, we no longer are surprised by the cruelty, even sadism, carried out in the name of God.

Kimball's other characteristics of religion turned toxic include: (1) an emphasis on blind obedience; (2) a structure of belief wherein the end justifies any means; and (3) declarations of "holy war" (moral cruelty, by its more common name). From antiquity to the present, the photographic record ensuing from this collage of ameaningful assumptions is appalling. Consider this account of one of Christianity's "triumphant victories" during the Crusades:

> On July 15, 1099, the crusaders breached the defenses of Jerusalem and began slaughtering wantonly. They set fire to the Great Synagogue, where the Jews had gathered for safety, burning them alive. They stormed the Noble Sanctuary (or Temple Mount), where thousands of Muslims had gathered that Friday for prayers. Fleeing into the al-Aqsa Mosque, the Muslims paid a huge ransom in return for guarantees of their safety. It didn't matter. The next day they were all slaughtered. Raymond of Agiles summarized the 'triumphant' scene:

'Some of our men (and this was more merciful) cut off the
heads of their enemies; others shot them with arrows, so
that they fell from the towers; others tortured them longer
by casting them into flames. Piles of heads, hands and feet
were to be seen in the streets of the city. It was necessary to
pick one's way over the bodies of men and horses. But these
were small matters compared to what happened at the temple
of Solomon, a place where religious services are ordinarily
chanted. What happened there? If I tell the truth, it will exceed
your powers of belief. So let it suffice to say this much at
least, that in the temple and portico of Solomon, men rode in
blood up to their knees and the bridle reins. Indeed, it was
a just and splendid judgment of God, that this place should
be filled with the blood of unbelievers, when it had suffered
so long from their blasphemies. Now that the city was taken
it was worth all our previous labors and hardships to see the
devotion of the pilgrims at the Holy Sepulcher. How they
rejoiced and exulted and sang the ninth chant to the Lord'
(in Kimball 2002: 163-164).

Ancient history? Yes, and no. In March, 2002, a recording of a private
conversation between Richard Nixon and populist evangelist Billy Graham
was released, wherein Graham speaks of Jews "ruining the country" and
suggests that Nixon, should he be re-elected, could "do something" about
that (in Kimball 2002: 137).

If religion is indeed an "opiate of the masses," it is a palliative
that functions in this manner: It ameliorates the pain and anxiety stemming
from the uncertainty of life, the certainty of death and the meaning of life
and death. It does, so, however, at great cost: the transformation of one's
own uncertainty into an aggressive, deadly need to establish one's truth
as absolute. . . for all. (My daddy really is the best daddy in the world.)
"Individuals, feeling helpless on their own, turn to their group for identity
and connection" (Deaux, Reid, Mizrahi & Cotting 1999: 182).

It may be the case, however, that pain, anxiety, and uncertainty
are necessary to understanding the world, to making volitional choices,
and to developing character and integrity. This heightened desire to avoid

existential anxiety and uncertainty, understandable though it may be, contributes to the toxic elements inherent in religious systems. And like the opiates, the relief from uncertainty can become addictive. The addicted person is seldom aware of the effects of the addiction; the addictive state clouds the mind and tricks the person into thinking that he is coherent, into thinking everything is okay. But everything is not okay. In like manner, "the loss of one's myth involves a profoundly disorienting loss of identity; it not only regulates behavior and enshrines knowledge, but it also constrains the perception of reality and channels the thought skills of its adherents. . . " (Donald 1991: 258).

One offshoot of the "absolute certainty of my one way" assumption is an increased likelihood of ameaningful thinking and justified cruelty. We are considerably more likely to harm others, feeling morally righteous, even holy, as we do so. The irony, however, is this: We may also be doing harm to ourselves, engaging not just in destruction, but self-destruction. How? This same system of meaning, which began as a quest to unify threads of experience into a tapestry of meaning, has emerged as a straightjacket instead. Rather than serving an integrative function in the dynamic, ongoing quest that is life itself, *all* answers are in, *all* issues are settled. It is finished. Rather than serving in a liberating manner wherein "the truth can set one free," the myth has solidified the boundaries of meaning. I now perceive my religion, and life itself, in terms of constraint, limitation and obligation. Ameaningful religion has terminated in an "escape from freedom," to borrow Erich Fromm's language. In Elie Wiesel's words, "all ready made answers, all seemingly unalterable certainties serve only to provide a good conscience to those who like to sleep and live peaceably. To avoid spending a lifetime tracking down truth, one pretends to have found it" (1972: 241). Actually, we may say that one "knows" to have found truth, because at this stage, the pretense has long since been buried beneath conscious awareness.

Is our choice, then, one of adopting a myth of certainty, or facing life with no system of meaning at all? Not at all; in fact, we hold that an attempt to live a life devoid of any system of meaning, any life narrative, constitutes an ameaningful approach in its own right. What we mean is this: Rather than offering a single, unambiguous answer to life itself, religion can and often does offer a way to embrace life—not solve it in algorithmic fashion. In lived religion one discovers a way of life, rather than adopts a set of rules. Becoming part of a tradition within which one can authentically grapple with life provides an important context—a crucible for spiritual development. But if we fail to make the tradition our own, if we just accept what the ancients said—rather than add our own voice to the story—then the tension between life as we experience it and life as tradition has rendered it can easily lead to anger, to violence, to harm. For example, how do we in the twenty-first century understand the idea that one should stone a disobedient child to death as it says in the Tanach? What does it mean to us today to turn the other cheek, to love one's enemy? In what way shall the meek inherit the earth when faced with a neighborhood bully, let alone a tyrant hell-bent on genocide? Struggling with these questions, and others like them, requires that we keep our traditions living and that we participate in the making of narrative.

Another paradox, then, may be this: Although some dimension of the human psyche may seem to need closure and certainty, another part of who we are seems to require searching, an ongoing quest.

At its best religion provides a meaningful framework for asking important questions without necessarily providing absolutely certain answers, yet without resorting to abject relativism. It can offer a context within which to think about the difficult decisions that we make every day and to ponder the meaning of events as they happen to us and around us. For example, what should one say when visiting a house of mourning? What if one talks about loss in terms of a person going to a "better place?" This might be comforting to an individual who has the same kind of belief system. But if mourners fail to believe it, this might lead them to be angry at themselves about their lack of faith in God. Or it might lead them to "blasphemy," that is condemning God for taking the person, even if to a better place. Or it might lead the person to a loss of faith in God.

And suppose that a person does not believe in an afterlife even if, at the age of nine, he had walked down the aisle of a Southern Baptist church and asked to be baptized. What is his response to be, nearly forty years later, to the death of his three-month-old son? Are there any non-religious narratives of meaning that will make sense of this non-sense? Perhaps not. In the final analysis, there may exist limits to language, to narrative, to myth. In such instances, it is such words as those penned by Elie Wiesel that take us as far as we are able to go. There may be some experiences that cannot be understood, or shared, but simply lived:

> 'Certain experiences may be transmitted by language, others—more profound —by silence; and then there are those that cannot be transmitted, not even by silence.' Never mind. Who says that experiences are made to be shared? They must be lived. That's all. And who says that truth is made to be revealed? It must be sought. That's all (Wiesel 1972: 240).

Part Three

Ameaning
and the Future

Chapter 8

Moral Cruelty: Sketch of a Theory

Few people nowadays know what man is. Many sense this ignorance and die the more easily because of it . . . I do not consider myself less ignorant than most people . . . I have been and still am a seeker, but I have ceased to question stars and books; I have begun to listen to the teachings my blood whispers to me. My story is not a pleasant one; it is neither sweet nor harmonious as invented stories are; it has the taste of nonsense and chaos, of madness and dreams like the lives of all men who stop deceiving themselves.

—Herman Hesse, *Demian*

Generally we are not encouraged to think about nonsense and chaos, or madness and dreams. Rather, logic, conformity and rationality are the order of the day. Rigidly constructed social edifices make our world feel safe and predictable—even as they help to perpetuate a social order that tolerates, allows or even encourages cruelty. If, as we have argued, certain social structures serve to justify personal agendas that also enhance social status, then our unwitting embrace of *moral cruelty* becomes less mysterious: We create moral narratives (at least in part) to provide a cloak of decency for otherwise harmful acts.

By examining moral cruelty in its many guises and by exposing the ameaningful thinking that underlies the creation and maintenance of morally cruel systems, we have sought to provide a lens through which to see the various ways that ordinary human beings seek to control, suppress and harm others—while concurrently perceiving themselves as good. Morally cruel acts succeed when their cruelty is effectively camouflaged, both from us and from others. By focusing on the moral rationales for our behavior, we fail to perceive the harm inherent in the act and instead justify our acts with socially sanctioned rectitude. Our morally cruel acts are then perceived as legitimate, defensible, in some instances even holy.

It is in the personal and cultural *perception* of morally cruel acts that we find the crux of the problem. As individuals and groups we strive to convince ourselves of the rightness of our actions. If our behavior corresponds with acceptable standards, we need not consider its effects on others. Individual and cultural perceptions of events assign them their meaning. In one culture generosity becomes a virtue, miserliness a vice. In another culture the accumulation of material wealth is highly valued while poverty suggests moral bankruptcy. Culture provides the ground against which we perceive the moral figure.

The personal and social perception of behavior incorporates two distinct vantage points: that of the person who is engaging in acts of cruelty but simultaneously perceiving the acts as moral, and that of individuals not directly involved in the acts but who also fail to perceive the inherent cruelty. Individuals may then justify their cruel acts both on the basis of their preexisting moral belief systems and because the reactions of those in their social group sanction the behavior. The rightness of individual behavior is determined by group perception, and the actions of the group are assigned meaning according to a shared narrative.

Consider the following illustration. Recently, a nature program broadcast on *The Discovery Channel* documented the lives of zebras on the African veldt. Prior to the beginning of the program and at intervals throughout the channel cautioned parents that some of the footage in the program was not suitable for children. The upsetting portion of the program depicted a rare clip of a young, orphaned zebra foal. Female zebras, we are told, will not adopt or care for the offspring of other zebras. This particular foal had been parentless for several days, its mother having died shortly after delivery. Experiencing great hunger and the resulting distress, the foal began braying loudly and continuously. After a time several large male zebras from the herd encircled the distressed orphan as if to protect it. Instead, and without warning, the adult males began to kick the foal furiously and relentless—until it lay dead.

If we use this event as a basis for exploring the anatomy of moral cruelty, what do we see? If, for a moment, we pretend that the zebras possess the capability and willingness to justify their actions, what would they say? How would they account for their seemingly brutal actions?

Perhaps their answer would incorporate a human adage: The needs of the many outweigh the needs of the few. Defense of the herd entails sacrifice. Our now talkative zebras might add that the distressing braying of the orphaned foal was attracting predators to an easy meal. As the foal attracted predators to itself, it was also attracting predators to the entire herd, placing everyone at risk. "As harsh as this seems," our striped spokesmen might continue, "the sacrifice was necessary for the preservation of the group. It might seem cruel to you, but it was a morally necessary act to us."

Such explanations illustrate the cognitions that accompany behavior, the reasons we offer ourselves for our actions. All behavior other than the purely reflexive is by definition motivated, and motivation presupposes an emotional component. Indeed, the word *emotion* originates in the Latin for "to move." In many instances we are unaware of the emotional component of our motivations, even as we concurrently create cognitive explanations for our behaviors. With this in mind, let us return to our zebras.

Assuming that the zebras could describe the emotions they felt as they were "performing their duty," what feelings would they report? If we use human experience as a guidepost, we would assume that a range of possible reactions is possible. The zebras might report feeling emotionally devastated at having killed the foal. It is possible that feelings of sadness, grief and guilt would accompany them as long as the memory of the event persisted. Another possibility however, is that rather than focusing on the act itself, our zebras might instead focus on the moral justification for their act. They might see themselves as dutiful, even heroic players in a larger drama, having used their physical strength to protect the herd. As a result, rather than sadness or guilt they might experience pride and satisfaction in a job well done. In this instance we have something akin to what Lieutenant Plummer reported after the bombing of Trang Bang—pride of accomplishment. In neither instance can we say that the aggressors consciously enjoyed killing. Rather, the positive emotional experiences they experienced flowed from the fact that their behaviors were culturally sanctioned, that they were living up to expectations inherent in filling a specific social role. As a result the focus would be on the *outcome* of the actions (protecting the herd, defending the Vietnamese), rather than on the *actions* themselves (and the *harmful consequences* of those actions).

When the victims of malevolent actions are valued by the society, the harm is not tolerated. However, when the victim represents a socially sanctioned target of aggression, cruelty is not only tolerated, it is justified. This is not to suggest that the behavior of the zebras is in any way directly analogous with morally cruel behavior in humans. Offering such simple one-dimensional explanations for human behavior would almost certainly be in error. Typically humans do not engage in blind cruelty, but rather in cleverly selected patterns of cruelty that can be aligned with prevailing cultural norms. With acts of human cruelty, the role of cognition is critical.

The Human Triad and the Creation of Ameaningful Morality

Tripartite models of the mind have dominated our attempts to explain human mental functioning since earliest recorded history. From the triune god of Christianity to Freud's id-ego-superego structural model to the cognition-emotion-action model of modern cognitive psychology, we find three-part explanations of psychological phenomena everywhere. In examining the psychological and developmental origins of ameaningful moral systems, we rely here on the self-object-affect model of modern developmental psychoanalysis. To begin our exploration, though, we need first examine the relative roles that cognition, affect and behavior play in the creation of psychological experience and, by extension, the creation of the self.

Historically, the problem in detangling the various roles that affect, cognition and behavior play in the development of personal belief systems has been in determining where to begin. To consider cognition, affect and behavior as separate entities perpetuates a widely held but demonstrably false assumption. It is increasingly apparent that all three are inextricably linked and that the apparent confusion stems from linguistic artifacts. Despite increased awareness that cognition, emotion and behavior form an integrated whole, researchers have made little headway in articulating the links among them.

In his book *Emotional Intelligence* (1995), Daniel Goleman made a valiant attempt to integrate two of these components, emotion and cognition. Unfortunately, although he reached for a synthesis, an outmoded model of an antagonistic emotion-cognition relationship underlies his reasoning. Goleman maintains that cognition's essential function lies in mastering the vicissitudes of emotional experience. Thus, once again we are left with an inadequate master-slave model of the cognition-emotion relationship.

The failure of the master-slave model of cognition and emotion to adequately account for human psychological functioning does not, of course, provide support for the opposite assertion: devaluing reason and championing irrational or nonrational causes of behavior. Instead, we prefer to consider the failure of this historically dominant model as an opportunity to ask some fundamental questions about the relations among cognition, affect and action. Where do we begin our investigation into the relations among these three phenomena? Where does the nexus of these phenomena lie? How does each relate to the development of ameaningful moral structures? Is moral cruelty best understood as a cognitive, emotional or behavioral phenomenon? Until a starting point is defined, no further inquiry is possible.

An apt analogy occurs in Kurt Vonnegut's *Mother Night*. The central character in the novel, Howard Campbell, no longer knows who he is or where his life is going. After years as an American double agent playing the role of a Nazi propagandist, he can no longer determine which of his roles is "real." Suddenly, years after the war has ended, he finds himself frozen, standing in a New York City street unable to move. Vonnegut informs the reader that Campbell is not frozen by guilt or fear or anger. Rather, he is frozen because he has no way to decide what he should do next. He has no reason to take a step in one direction as opposed to any other. He has no guiding preference, no orientation, and no direction.

Objectively such an experience is absurd. If, as empirical science argues, every event, every behavior is the result of an endless chain of causal events, then every behavior leads naturally and inevitably to another. Running out of causes is quite impossible. Subjectively, however, the behavior makes perfect sense. When viewed through the lens of Campbell's own existential emptiness, the inevitability of his confusion is immediately apparent. Indeed, given his psychological circumstances, making recourse to the subjective nature of his experience is the only method by which Campbell's behavior may be understood.

Unfortunately the examination of the subjective aspects of mental life ("experience as lived") is no longer a widely practiced approach to the study of human psychology. Aspiring to become a hard science like physics and chemistry, psychology has embraced a logical-positivist experimental model of inquiry that limits investigation to subjects that can be observationally-defined. The result has been increasing acceptance of laboratory analogues and quasi-experimental designs as the only acceptable lens through which human psychology may be studied. Begging for the moment any discussion of the appropriateness of this model for the investigation of human *psychology* (as opposed to human behavior or human brain function), let us turn our attention to that bulwark of scientific investigation: objectivity.

As Merleau-Ponty poignantly observed, "Empiricism cannot see that we need to know what we are looking for, otherwise we would not be looking for it, while intellectualism fails to see that we need to be ignorant of what we are looking for, or. . . we should not be searching" (1962: 28). Similarly, Michael Polanyi noted that, ". . . to look at the universe objectively, one would need to pay equal attention to portions of equal mass [which] would result in a lifelong preoccupation with interstellar dust, and not in a thousand million lifetimes would the turn come to give man even a second's notice" (1958: 3). To be truly objective would, like Vonnegut's character, render us frozen.

Objectivity is thus a chimera. If nothing else, to function as humans we must choose a starting point, some place to which we turn our attention within this expanding universe of infinite stellar dust. And there exists no *a priori* rationale for choosing one point of departure over another. To know where to begin we must integrate our own psychological values into our perceptual field. We have to consider the subjective meaning of our beliefs and our actions.

So, to return to our original problem, where does this leave us? It leaves us back with Lieutenant Plummer. What we can say empirically is that some people consider Lieutenant Plummer's actions more important than his reasons for acting, while others will say that his reasons are more important than his actions. Some look at his actions and see a necessary evil. Others see only evil. The difference is one of perspective, which suggests an essential perceptual foundation to morality. Morality is sensibility–dependent.

Toward a Developmental Model of Moral Cruelty

Considerable evidence supports the contention that humans, like other social animals, are motivated to seek contact with others (Bowlby 1969; Konner 1983). Indeed, our very sense of self originates in the psychological internalization of our early attachments (Ainsworth, Blehar, Waters & Wall 1978). The mental representations we have of ourselves (and of our selves in relation to other selves) form the foundation of our sense of who we are and what it means to be us.

The self that we develop depends primarily on the quality of the attachments we experience as children. This is not to say that all personality development (or all moral development, for that matter) occurs in childhood. Rather, the foundation for our sense of ourselves in the world seems to be laid down at an early age (Erikson 1963; Shaver & Rubenstein 1980; Sroufe & Waters 1977). Later elaboration of both our sense of self and of others occurs as a result of the experiences we have throughout life. However, because these experiences are based in large part on perceptions gathered through the lens of our preexisting understanding of self and others, they at best make contributions to preexisting self structures, rarely creating wholly new structures of themselves. Thus, the quality of our childhood attachments provides a fundamental basis for our perceptions of self and other throughout our lives (Bowlby 1973; Hazan & Shaver 1990; Tidwell, Reis & Shaver 1996).

Moral development occurs within the context of our attachments to and relationships with others (deWaal 1996). Speaking of morality as divorced from the context of human relationships simply makes no sense. Attachment relationships that provide safety and a sense of belonging create, in turn, a sense of self free from fears of impending disintegration, of not continuing to exist—a primary source of human anxiety. Conditional or insecure attachments create the conditions for a sense of self plagued by disintegration anxieties and overwhelmed by fears of abandonment (Cohen & Sherwood 1991; Mikulincer 1997; Mikulincer & Orbach 1995). As a result, anxiety is experienced whenever there exists a threat to the sense of self, activating fears of disintegration and abandonment. And, as we discussed earlier, research on motivated social perception consistently finds that threats to the self-image prompt the activation of the prejudices and stigmatizing stereotypes that typify morally cruel behavior (Fein et al. 2003). Morally cruel behavior and the ameaningful moral reasoning that underlies it may thus be seen as responses to the anxiety created by threats to the self-image.

It is important to understand that insecure attachments and concerns with the integrity of the self are not experiences limited to those with psychopathology. Rather, in every instance human development is marked by (at least occasional) failures of attachment and occasions of anxiety. Thus the experiences of anxiety and the automatic activation of ameaningful moral belief structures that prompt moral cruelty are ubiquitous in human life. None of us is free of the tinge of existential dread that prompts unreasonable moral behavior or the developmental experiences that place us at risk of such behavior. The result, to borrow a phrase, is the moral cruelty of everyday life.

Chapter Nine

The Final Analysis

with contributing author Michael Arfken

Exploitation must not be seen as such. It must be seen as benevolence. Persecution preferably should not need to be invalidated as the figment of a paranoid imagination; it should be experienced as kindness. . . . In order to sustain our amazing images of ourselves as God's gift to the vast majority of the starving human species, we have to interiorize our violence upon ourselves and our children, and to employ the rhetoric of morality to describe this process.

—R.D. Laing

The theories of Milton Friedman gave him the Nobel Prize; they gave Chile General Pinochet. *—Edward Galeano*

I have never been able to conceive how any rational being could propose happiness to himself from the exercise of power over others.

—Thomas Jefferson, Slaveholder

It is not possible to commit deforestation, or any other mass atrocity—mass murder, genocide, mass rape, the pervasive abuse of women or children, institutionalized animal abuse, imprisonment, wage slavery, systematic impoverishment, ecocide—without first convincing yourself and others that what you're doing is beneficial. You must have, as Dr. Robert Jay Lifton has put it, a "claim to virtue."

—Derrick Jensen

Honest discourse is the first and most important step in stopping destruction. *—Derrick Jensen*

Five years have passed since we began work on this volume. In 1998, as the dawn of a new century and a new millennium drew near, we were disturbed as we surveyed the range of topics that captured social attention. Ominous threats about the "Y2K" computer bug and its potential effect on world economies were forecast daily. New gene therapies for age-old diseases—and even talk of "solving" the problem of aging (and death)—surfaced more prominently. Technological answers to our oldest questions were announced, as we communicated effortlessly and instantly even with people we have never met, around the world. Globalization of markets and the emergence of a worldwide market were heralded as signs of a world in transformation. "Most influential person" lists were proffered ad infinitum, as the "great man in history" paradigm continued to shape our view of collective destiny—with accommodation of a "great woman" contribution here and there. What captured our attention, however, was what had *failed* to snare *attention* during this collective retrospection: the current status of human and social development as we prepared to enter the twenty-first century—the question of whether and how we had advanced as human beings.

Even now, ask anyone how the world might be better in fifty years, one hundred years, five hundred years, or another millennium, and the answer almost certainly revolves around expected technological advances and almost never around imminent moral, social, or psychological improvements. This tendency is reflected in such scholarly works as *The Next Fifty Years: Science in the First Half of the Twenty-First Century*, and in such popular culture media as "Star Trek," "Star Wars," and "The Matrix"—wherein the technology of weaponry has advanced, but the foibles of humanity appear all too familiar.

We chose to respond with a counterpoint, an assertion that the real crisis for the future is not Y2K nor technological advancement. Rather, a defining crisis for humanity and future prospects for all human beings center around the question of whether we have advanced in areas of life defined by kindness, empathy, civility, character, community. It is for that reason that we began this book by pointing to another "record" established in the twentieth-century: more human beings were systematically exterminated than in any century prior.

Since those initial questions we have lived through the transition into the new millennium, and soon to follow, the events of 9/11 and its aftermath. It is as if we witnessed moral cruelty crystallize before our eyes, as sentence by sentence we attempted to capture harm done —but cloaked with a veil of the good—and render it visible. Let us begin with December 31, 1999, and connect that evening to our analysis of the orphaned zebra (Chapter 8).

It is the eve of a new year, a new century, a new millennium. My wife and I (CJF) are living in Bucharest, Romania, where we have lived for over a year and during which we have spent a great deal of time in the country's orphanages. In one orphanage, where even the physical facilities and addressing of physical needs (feeding and clothing) was inadequate, an image (obtained as a follow-up piece, *Turning Point*, Ugent, 1999) comes into focus:

> The kids in this Romanian home got one meal a day—a bowl of watered-down broth with pieces of bread in it. They bathed once a month, in dirty water with no soap. There were too many children to each bed and too few caregivers: Some children, starved for stimulation, beat their heads against the wall. . . .

> [In one institution in Siret:] Most of the children sent there had a medical condition, like hemophilia or recurrent seizures; others were blind or handicapped or had something as relatively benign as a learning disability.

> The children were, in every sense of the word, forgotten. Slapped with the label "irrecuperable"—meaning lost cause— they were destined to remain institutionalized for life. Most died young from easily treatable medical problems—not just those they came in with, but also problems contracted from malnutrition or the filth.

From one of the "better" orphanages, here's another photograph: A young child, twelve months old, who has been fed well and clothed, but who has received less than three minutes of human stimulation per day. As we walk into a room where 12-15 babies are housed, we see many of them on all fours, rhythmically rocking themselves as they attempt to fall asleep. We turn to see one twelve-month-old, already developmentally-delayed, begin to forcefully pound his head against the side of the wooden crib. Due to lack of stimulation by touch, even his tactile sense has not developed properly. Thus, he creates more intense stimulation, pounding his own head ever harder, just to register something in his sensory system.

As easy as it may be for many of us to perceive cruelty in the treatment of children in Siret, the conditions depicted here survived into the new millennium. Thus, as we awoke on New Year's Day with nary a trace of the great "Y2K doomsday collapse" in evidence, we were faced with one over-riding question: Why is so little attention devoted to these tiny victims and the millions of children in deplorable conditions world-wide?

As we continue to confront the cruelty inflicted on the children in Romania and around the world, we note the admonition of Alice Miller:

> Every act of cruelty, no matter how brutal and shock-ing, has traceable antecedents in its perpetrator's past (1983: ix).

> The scorn and abuse directed at the helpless child as well as the suppression of vitality, creativity, and feeling in the child and in oneself permeate so many areas of our life that we hardly notice it anymore. Almost every-where we find the effort marked by varying degrees of intensity and by the use of various coercive measures, to rid ourselves as quickly as possible of the child within us. . . (1983: 58).

In making sense of our treatment of orphans, our dilemma brings us to the crux of moral cruelty. While many people react to the plight of the young zebra as it is pounded to death, our reaction to the conditions of human beings across the street and around the world seems understated—at times nonexistent. While a possible "Y2K" crisis was so widely publicized as to make one ill upon hearing the phrase yet again, the actual plight of children languishing in an orphanage apparently failed the social litmus test for "crisis." If we can still readily ignore, tolerate or even defend the conditions of a Romanian orphanage, what else are we tolerating in terms of the daily doses of cruelty?

The answer to that question revolves around the concept of attention. From the psychological vantage point, moral cruelty—ameaningful at its roots—represents a *failure of attention*: By attending to pre-manufactured rationales for our actions, rather than noting their implicit harm, we fail to perceive the sadistic component of our behavior. Because the harm is hidden, we may say that we hide the reality of cruelty from ourselves. Thus, the question of whether moral cruelty will define the future hinges on the question of attention and the attendant issue of self-deception.

Self-Deception as Failure of Attention

It should be safe to say that everyone has experienced a new insight or understanding at some point in life. Such insights are invariably accompanied by the recognition that some prior belief or perception was incorrect. This phenomenon leads us to a general principle of perceptual change: If what we once believed to be true we now see as false, then might there not be other tenets to which we currently cling that may also prove to be false? If what we once perceived as permissible we now perceive as harmful, then in which of my current perceptions might a harmful element be hidden?

An attendant fear accompanies these questions, a fear that we must manage. One of the prime terror management strategies seems to be avoidance of potentially conflicting information—an intentional narrowing of one's perceptual field. Festinger's theory of cognitive dissonance (1957) explains motivated cognitive avoidance in this manner: Individuals are likely to reject potentially available information if that information contradicts currently-held ideas, beliefs, or feelings, because in doing so we avoid the unpleasant state of dissonance (internal discord).

Even prior to Festinger, Sigmund Freud had argued that incoming information— whether from external reality or information retrieved from one's internal memory system—is likely to be diverted, transformed, or deleted on the way to conscious awareness. In a manner that anticipated later cognitive theory, Freud postulated cognitive "censors" that oppose movement of threatening material into awareness. Once information is designated as "threatening," the material is either transformed, or barred from conscious awareness altogether, by those psychic filters. In other words, the censors filter out information likely to provoke anxiety while allowing benign information to continue along the way. There appears to be a distinct bargain in the making: The range of possible experiences is narrowed and *attention to potentially unpleasant or upsetting thoughts and feelings is diminished*, in order to reduce the likelihood of experiencing pain or anxiety.

The immediate relevance of Festinger's and Freud's constructs to the phenomenon of moral cruelty should be readily apparent: Thoughts, memories, and ideas that might produce pain or anxiety are omitted from individual awareness. Each lacuna, each perceptual gap or cognitive omission, prevents an accurate or complete perception of reality. But because we are seldom (if ever) aware of the lacuna, we may simultaneously believe consciously that our cognitions are accurate.

"Self-knowledge in Freud's sense is not an intellectual process alone, but simultaneously an affective process, as it was already for Spinoza. It is not only knowledge by the brain, but also knowledge by the heart. Knowing oneself means gaining increasing insight, intellectually and affectively, in heretofore secret parts of one's psyche" (Fromm 1973: 56). Where knowledge of self is lacking, we may rather easily adhere to and focus attention on our beliefs, while failing to perceive harm that ensues from our actions.

Consider, for example, an advertising theme that announces: "You are what you wear." Let's say that we hear this message, compare it to what we already know about ourselves—our beliefs, values, attitudes, and so on—and ultimately reject the information on the basis that it is both discrepant and false. Then, we "forget" the message that we just heard. Are we thereby guilty of self-deception?

Later that day, someone walks up to us and says: "You all are wearing Pikey sneakers, which were manufactured in a sweatshop. You are oppressors of innocent people." We acknowledge that the sneakers are of that brand and that we are wearing them. We reject the accusation of being "oppressors," however, because it is discrepant from views that we already hold regarding the "moral goodness" of our self systems. As for information regarding the conditions under which Pikey sneakers are made, we simply screen that information from awareness; we "know nothing" about their manufacture. Are we now guilty of self-deception?

What are the differences in these two examples? Can one be a legitimate case of self-affirmation, the other a bona fide instance of self-deception? Is either conducive to acts of moral cruelty? Our answer is in the affirmative.

In the first example, we consider the possibility that "we are what we wear" and test it against other beliefs that we hold, for example, ideas that we are what we eat, we are what we think, we are what we feel, we are what we do, and so on. After engaging in a process of reflective, meaningful thinking, we determine that there are a number of life facets that go into the making of self-identity, and that while clothing may be one reflection of self, it is clearly not the only one or even the most important one. The determination of how we handle the message, "you are what you wear," is made not from a basis of fear, of avoidance of dissonance, or immediate censoring of the message altogether. Rather, we examined the discrepant message for a period of time sufficient to test its veracity in an engaged, meaningful fashion—and even remained willing to revisit the issue should we find information that challenges our current reading (e.g., discovering that the largest expenditures in our personal financial budget are allocated to clothing).

In the second example, we acknowledge that we are wearing Pikey sneakers but refuse to acknowledge even *the possibility* that in doing so we have contributed to oppression of other human beings. When we reject the label of "oppressors" in the absence of additional query or efforts, then we are engaged in filtering information that we do not wish to hear—consciously, unconsciously, or on a continuum that includes both—in order to avoid the unpleasantness inherent in the recognition. This premature closure contains the fear, the terror, of seeing the relationship between our actions and the harm they impose on others, and it avoids the effort and energy essential to meaningful reflection on a particular engagement with reality. It as an understanding of precisely this self-deception strategy that led Simone Weil to a series of insights that connect premature cognitive closure and the failure of attention to the infliction of harm (evil). Speaking of our general aversion to true attention, Weil asks, "Is not evil analogous to illusion?" Then, by way of answering her questions, she states that all wrong translations, absurdities, faulty connections, cherished illusions and misunderstandings "are due to the fact that thought has seized upon some idea too hastily, and being thus prematurely blocked, is not open to the truth" (in Frost and Bell-Metereau 1998: 55-57).

Like Simone Weil, Sartre was unwilling to let us off the hook. He argued that for cognitive censors to work effectively, the individual must "know" the truth—at some level. To successfully deceive ourselves, Sartre continued, we must pre-reflectively be aware that we are acting in bad faith; the locus of control for bad faith lies within the individual (Sartre 1956).

We concur with the conclusion reached by Weil and Sartre. A human being is not predestined to live a life primarily characterized by denial and deception. To the contrary, a person may choose as life project the careful, painstaking path of avowing explicitly all of one's engagements with the world. Articulating one's engagement with the world can be understood as similar to explicitly communicating an idea to another individual: To articulate one's engagement with that person is to make one's motivations apparent to that individual. In like manner, to articulate one's engagement to oneself, to "reflect" on one's being-in-the-world, is to make one's motivations apparent to self.

In stark contrast, the individual engaged in self-deception refuses to spell out his thoughts or behaviors; conversely, he refuses to avow himself as one who does not spell out his engagements. With each omission or disavowal, it seems, the project of deception becomes more rooted in the potential for harm. Note here the almost perfect parallel between the psychological and social domains. An individual who relies heavily on avoidance and censoring of information is the one whose potential for harm increases exponentially; a political-social entity that relies heavily on avoidance and censoring of information is the one most likely to cause harm.

Given the relative ease of deceiving oneself and the apparent difficulty of achieving a self characterized by an unerring engagement in meaningful reasoning, what is the primary stumbling block to sustained attention? At the level of the individual the challenge may be this: Is it possible to attend to one's own motivations and the consequences of one's actions rigorously and *simultaneously*? That is, is it possible to look into both a full-view mirror and a full-length window *at the same time*?

If cognitive psychologists are correct, human beings are capable of divided attention to an extent, but only to an extent. At each moment of existence we are presented with a range of stimuli that far exceeds our capacity of attention; attention is, by definition, *selective* attention. As we turn our focus from one emphasis to the next, the contents of consciousness shift imperceptibly in pursuit, relegating what was in awareness to the realm of memory. And as memory researchers warn us, when we attend to material previously stored we reconstruct its contents in accordance with present knowledge—in a manner more fitting our current attentive gaze.

At the psychological level, the antidote to self-deception is to remain vigilant in one's perception, to attend in good faith to the inner world of self while simultaneously attending to, avowing, and articulating one's engagement with the world. To continually remain alert for the possibility of deception, to maintain attention to self and world, becomes the prime prerequisite of meaningful thinking and by extension meaningful morality. Attention functions much like the conductor of one's intrapersonal orchestra and is a necessary condition to the capacity for meaningful thought. When there is no conductor, ameaningful thinking fills the void. A conductor-less symphony of moral cruelty is very likely to follow.

> [It] is only our own fear that sets us apart. . . . [Humans] are struggling to be sane, struggling to live in harmony with our surroundings, but it's really hard to let go. And so we lie, destroy, rape, murder, experiment, and extirpate, all to control *this wildly uncontrollable symphony*, and failing that, to destroy it (Jensen 2000: 75-76; italics added).

The puzzling paradox of self-deception is that it seems to bestow short-term benefits to the self (maintain consistency, avoid anxiety of discrepant information, able to turn attention elsewhere, etc.), concurrently exacting a price to others, to relatedness. We may say that the greater an individual's proclivity for self-deception, the more pronounced that person's capacity to harm others—without even perceiving the actions as harmful. It may be that the most pervasive human cruelty is cruelty that has been deceptively camouflaged; in other words, the most widespread form of harmfulness is that which we term *moral cruelty*. By the time that we witness the deaths of over six million Jews, notice Romanian babies living in concentration camp conditions, or see the sweat shop conditions wherein our favorite sneakers are manufactured, we may finally turn our attention and notice actions themselves. But we may still fail to perceive the web of deception that spun the crucial crucible for carrying out such atrocious substitutes for relatedness in the first place. We close the gate long after the horses have escaped.

Moral Cruelty And The Crucible Of Social Reality

It may seem as if we are advancing an "individualistic" theory of morality. We are not. Although we do pinpoint the locus of control of attention and meaningful moral reasoning within the person, we situate the person within the crucible of social reality. A child who grows up in the absence of a social context, like those rare cases of feral children, provides vivid evidence that neuropsychological development is inextricably linked to social development. When a number of children adopted from

Romanian orphanages after the age of five were administered brain scans, every single one of them had "black holes" evident in their brains—areas where little to no neural processing occurred. In an age where genetic and biologically-based determinism is rampant, the simple reality may be easily missed: Experience shapes our brains, and our brains (and associated cognitive functions) serve to navigate our experiences. The relationship is reciprocal, as is the relationship between the individual and society.

The future of moral cruelty depends upon the extent to which individuals develop a capacity for sustained attention and meaningful moral reasoning. The likelihood that individuals will do so depends upon the quality of community; in particular, home, school, education, workplace, and religion. While individualists may fail to see the important context that community affords, communitarians may fail to see that it is individuals that strike out and hit, or reach out and caress; that prematurely jump to a toxic conclusion, or reason meaningfully with the complexities of a moral dilemma; that choose to advance their own agenda, or choose to align their agenda with a greater good.

One way of understanding the general failure of individuals to attend to the consequences of their actions involves examining the current culture of moral narcissism. In his classic text, *The Anatomy of Human Destructiveness*, Erich Fromm argues that a primary source of destructiveness stems from the wounding of an individual's narcissism. He keenly observes the connection between narrow self focus and attention.

> A person, to the extent to which he is narcissistic, has a double standard of perception. Only he himself and what pertains to him has significance, while the rest of the world is more or less weightless or colourless, and because of this double standard the narcissistic person shows severe defects in judgment and lacks the capacity for [meaningful reasoning].

> When others wound his narcissism by slighting him, criticizing him, showing him up when he has said something wrong, defeating him in a game or on numerous other occasions, a narcissistic person usually reacts with intense anger or rage, whether or not he shows it or is even aware of it (Fromm 1973: 272-273).

In a book published shortly before the new millennium, Baumeister also struggles with the subtle distinction, of how to distinguish such positive individual characteristics as kindness, civility, caring, and integrity from the wanton individualism frequently critiqued—but rarely understood. In doing so, he pointed to a distinction that is beginning to surface in the psychological literature: positive or healthy self-esteem rooted in hard-won accomplishment and accountability versus an inflated sense of self-esteem in which one feels "entitled" simply because it is "me."

> Today, it is common to propose that low self-esteem causes violence, but the evidence shows plainly that this idea is false. Violent acts follow from high [inflated] self-esteem, not from low self-esteem.
>
> Actually, it is more precise to say that violence ensues when people feel that their favorable views of themselves are threatened or disputed by others. As a result, people whose self-esteem is high but lacks a firm basis in genuine accomplishment are especially prone to be violent, because they are most likely to have their narcissistic bubble burst.
>
> If you are like most people, you will feel like lashing out at anyone who says you are not as great as you thought. The more inflated your self-esteem is, the more common such encounters are (Baumeister 1999: 25-26).

Baumeister's reading of inflated self-esteem echo descriptions of untamed or unhealthy narcissism.

This line of reasoning is fine, as far as it goes, but it conceals some fatal flaws in the "damning of individualism" literature. What factors or conditions contribute to the development of unhealthy narcissism and rampant consumerism? Do these factors reside "within" the individual, or are they situated within the society, within the crucible of human development? Given the history of social and institutional harm (Nazism, Stalinism, and the litany of social genocides with which we began this work), might it not be time to move from the language of "individual versus community" to the language of "healthy community that fosters individuals of civility and integrity?"

As we consider these questions, we must remember that the problem is not that of single individuals driven to unhealthy narcissism by biological instinct or haphazard choice. To the contrary, it is the pervasive influence of media, government, religion, education, and corporate reality that stokes the fire of unhealthy individualism and consumerism. As Chomsky puts it, these social edifices of power intentionally sow the seeds of ameaning. It is no longer a question of power brokers (and their intellectual puppets) reflexively advocating control and coercion, but *intentionally* doing so.

> So in the twentieth century, there's a major current of American thought—in fact, it's probably the dominant current among people who think about these things (political scientists, journalists, public relations experts and so on)—which says that precisely because the state has lost the power to coerce [by blatant use of physical force], elites need to have more effective propaganda to control the public mind. That was Walter Lippmann's point of view, for example, to mention probably the dean of American journalists—he referred to the population as a 'bewildered herd': we have to protect ourselves from 'the rage and trampling of the bewildered herd.' And the way you do it, Lippmann said, is by what he called the 'manufacture of consent'—if you don't do it by force, you have to do it by the calculated 'manufacture of consent' (Chomsky 2002: 16).

In a society dominated by powerful social institutions churning away to manufacture consent, the communitarian solution—preaching at people to be more civic-minded and less individualistic—is not only insufficient, but to some extent compatible with the manufacture of ameaning.

First, let us repeat: We do see clearly the danger of untamed narcissism, narrow self-indulgence, and unbridled consumerism. The individual who focuses attention only through the filters of self-interest is eminently capable of moral cruelty. That said, we have developed our theory in terms of an even more puzzling aspect of this phenomenon: It is not only the perpetrator, but those who witness the cruelty who perceive the harm as moral. As we stated in the first chapter, in the context of an ameaningful moral system, viewing one's actions from different moral perspectives becomes unnecessary, indeed undesirable, if one's social group sanctions the actions. Put another way, perpetrating aggression becomes acceptable as long as it is done in a socially sanctioned manner against socially sanctioned targets.

For this reason, we conceptualize our theory not in terms of arguing the individual versus the community, but rather as the individual embedded within community. Fromm certainly understood the import of I–Others connectedness, and perceived a subtle distinction that many theorists have missed: Narcissism is a cloak that can cover more than the individual from which it emanates.

> [On the surface, narcissists can seem loyal to something outside themselves]: Thus, for instance, they will feel an inordinate admiration for their parents or for their children [or their country, race, etc., but the 'key' is to be found in the 'their'.]
>
> Group narcissism has important functions. In the first place, it furthers the solidarity and cohesion of the group, and makes manipulation easier by appealing to narcissistic prejudices. Secondly, it is extremely important. . . particularly to those who have few other reasons to feel proud and worthwhile . . . . Consequently, the degree of group narcissism is commensurate with the lack of real satisfaction in life.
>
> They receive their reward from feeling proud and satisfied to be serving such a worthy cause—and through enhanced prestige and promotion.
>
> Those whose narcissism refers to their group rather than to themselves as individuals are as sensitive as the individual narcissist, and they react with rage to any wound, real or imaginary, inflicted upon their group.
>
> Group narcissism is one of the most important sources of human [cruelty] (Fromm 1973: 273-276).

Fromm's analysis here gets to the core of moral cruelty, particularly his description of the way in which group narcissism promotes "feeling proud and satisfied"—even while inflicting harm. The depictions apply to parents beating their children "for their own good," to teachers who enforce regurgitation rather than facilitate discovery, to employers who treat workers as objects ("resources") to manipulate, to self-proclaimed patriots squelching dissent, and to religious adherents consigning to hell those who do not embrace their narrative. And the descriptions apply to the example with which we began this book: the case of Lieutenant Plummer.

Continuing his analysis, Fromm argues that aggressiveness, harming others, "is not just one *trait*, but part of a *syndrome*; . . . we find aggression regularly together with other traits in the system, such as strict hierarchy, dominance, class division, etc., [so] aggression is to be understood as part of the *social character*, not as an isolated behaviour trait" (Fromm 1973: 228). This conclusion conceals the "good news" that follows both his quest for the roots of human destructiveness, and ours:

> I believe I have demonstrated. . . that this destructiveness is neither innate, nor part of 'human nature', and that it is not common to all men. The question [is] what other and specifically human conditions are responsible for this potential viciousness (Fromm 1973: 246-247).

Beyond Moral Cruelty

The very premise of our theory presupposes that morality, moral intolerance in particular, can cloak harmfulness. Certainly this theme is implicit in Hawthorne's great novel, *The Scarlet Letter,* wherein Hester Prynn finds herself branded for transgressing the moral code, but emerges as the character truly possessive of meaningful morality. In advancing a perceptual theory of morality, we wish to align ourselves in the direction of Hester Prynn and away from the perspective of moral code as coercive branding iron.

The punitive, harmful renderings of morality *stem from attempts to encapsulate human beings.* It is for this reason, according to Fromm, that as civilization has increased, so too has the human tendency to harm.

It is as if we create stifling conditions that more resemble a prison or a zoo, and then wrongly assume that the highly organized nature of our edifice protects us from each other. In reading Fromm's statements here, remember that he completed much of his analysis decades ago, long before the United States succeeded in incarcerating more of its inhabitants than any nation on the planet.

> Observations show that primates in the wild show little aggression, while primates in the zoo can show an excessive amount of destructiveness. . . . [Kummer] found that the incidence of aggressive acts in the zoo was nine times as frequent in females and seventeen and a half times as frequent in adult males as it was in wild bands.

> This distinction is of fundamental importance for the understanding of human aggression because man thus far in his history has hardly ever lived in his 'natural habitat', with the exception of the hunters and food gatherers and the first agriculturalists down to the fifth millennium B.C. 'Civilized' man has always lived in the 'Zoo'—i.e., in various degrees of captivity and unfreedom—and this is still true, even in the most advanced societies (Fromm 1973: 148-149).

> Hence, man's hyper-aggression is not due to a greater aggressive *potential* but to the fact that aggression-producing *conditions* are much more frequent for humans than for animals living in their natural habitat. . . . It suggests that man, during most of his history, has lived in a zoo and not 'in the wild'—i.e., under the condition of liberty conducive to human growth and well-being (Fromm 1973: 251-252).

> The more fields were ploughed, the more marshes were drained, the more surplus could be produced. This new possibility led to one of the most fundamental changes in human history. *It was discovered that man could be used as an economic instrument, that he could be exploited, that he could be made a slave* (Fromm 1973: 223).

The move away from moral cruelty and toward meaningful morality lies in an opposite direction from confinement and coercion.

Continuing our focus on attention, we may say here that the restriction or constriction of attention underpins the propensity to harm in the name of the good. Cognitive research confirms that even when perceiving "physical" reality, we apprehend only those dimensions of the stimulus to which we have attended. As William James argued, a thing may be present to a person a thousand times, but if it goes completely unnoticed by the individual, it cannot be said to enter his experience (James 1890/ 1950). When we consider the perception of "social" reality, the stimulus is far more ambiguous and thus the contribution of the perceiver—and her habits of attention—are much more pronounced. As Gadamer (1987) states, the limitations of attention coupled with the ambiguity of social reality *necessitates* perceptual openness. Indeed, it is awareness of this flexibility that enables us to shift continually our perceptual gaze so that we can see ourselves and our world more fully (and accurately), and learn from the events that occur in our lives. In short, openness of attention moves in a direction opposite to that of self-deception.

For Gadamer, sustaining an openness to the constant possibility of changing and refining one's perspective or conceptual framework is a crucial feature of rationality itself. Both Gadamer and philosopher Alasdair MacIntyre define rationality as inclusive of *a willingness to admit the existence of better options, and a commitment to seek those options.* Keen awareness that one's current knowledge or perspective is always open to refutation or modification is not a basis for suspending confidence in the idea of reason; rather, it represents the very possibility of rational progress and runs counter to the propensity for self-deception.

It is not surprising, then, that Sigmund Koch characterized "*ameaningful thinking*" by such adjectives as "extrinsically–occasioned or forced, rigid, nonfluent, relatively formless, undifferentiated, grossly instrumental, unspontaneous, rote, [and] rule-bound" (Koch 1981). He concluded that such thinking generally perpetuates pseudoknowledge, a category that encompasses ignorance, propaganda and justifications of harm. In direct contrast, *meaningful thinking* is characterized by "an organic determination of the form and substance of thought by the properties of the object and the terms of the problem. In meaningful thinking, the mind caresses, flows joyously into, over, around the relational matrix defined by the problem, the object" (Koch 1981:79). Perceptual and cognitive openness comprises a necessary, though not sufficient first step in this direction.

If openness of attention comprises a first step by which to move beyond moral cruelty, the dialogical nature of perception provides the second. We bridge the self–other gap at the outset by recognizing that perception, ultimately, is transactional: We do not simply perceive, we perceive something, someone. It is here that Martin Büber is most instructive. Recognizing that one does not become "human" in isolation, Büber begins not from the point of "I," but from "I–Thou." If we originate our engagement with the world at "I–Thou," then we are already on our way to integrating cognitive, emotive, and behavioral dimensions of self and to bridging the individual–community antinomy.

Gadamer uses the term *Bildung* to discuss this facet of moral reasoning. Essentially, *Bildung* describes the process through which individuals and cultures enter a more widely delineated community, a more expansive and inclusive society. The "cultured" individual, then, is one who can place her life and concerns within a broader context, who perceives a broader horizon, who widens her cognitive perspective. She is a person who is not only familiar with but also interested in issues, problems and ways of life that may be quite distant from her own. It is not that differences must always be embraced or incorporated into one's own self or one's community. Rather, it is a purposeful recognition that even difference may enable a person to put his or her life and community in perspective.

At some level we intuitively know how cruel and uncompromising moral intolerance can be; we can read *The Scarlet Letter* and experience directly harm inflicted in the name of morality. One reason for this oppressive component, it seems, stems from viewing morality in terms of rules, codes and prohibitions. Morality comes to be viewed as an algorithm of coercive constriction, and individuals wishing to garner attention generally find that spouting "thou shalt nots" is a fairly simple game to play. However, coercion may also promote as well as curtail the likelihood of harm.

Consider, for instance, a scenario sketched by Simone Weil: Imagine passing a complex set of laws that prohibit individuals from ingesting disgusting and toxic substances, say gasoline, tainted beef and animal manure. Such prohibitions make no sense, because "not eating disgusting or dangerous things is not felt by the normal man to be any limitation of his liberty in the domain of food" (in Frost & Bell-Metereau 1998: 50). A person does not need or require "external constraint" in order to avoid eating such substances; rather, his understanding is such that he is not even motivated to consider such an action. Weil relies on this example in her discussion of liberty; in doing so, she anticipates a critical distinction articulated by Erich Fromm: "*freedom from*" versus "*freedom to.*" According to Fromm, our progression toward the former has been accompanied by a deepening lag in the latter:

> The history of civilization, from the destruction of Carthage and Jerusalem to the destruction of Dresden, Hiroshima, and the people, soil, and trees of Vietnam, is a tragic record of sadism and destructiveness (Fromm 1973: 226-227).

> It took over four hundred years to break down the medieval world and to free people from the most apparent restraints. But while in many respects the individual has grown, has developed mentally and emotionally, and participates in cultural achievements in a degree unheard-of before, the lag between "freedom from" and "freedom to" has grown too. The result of this disproportion between freedom from any tie and the lack of possibilities for the positive realization of freedom and individuality has led. . . to a panicky flight from freedom. . . (Fromm 1941: 36).

> [This means] growing isolation, insecurity, and thereby growing doubt concerning one's own role in the universe, the meaning of one's life, and with all that a growing feeling of one's own powerlessness and insignificance as an individual (Fromm 1941: 35).

> Freedom does not imply a lack of constraint, since any growth
> occurs only within a structure, and any structure requires con-
> straint (H. von Foerster 1970). What matters is whether the
> constraint functions primarily for the sake of another person
> or institution, or whether it is autonomous—i.e., that it results
> from the necessities of growth inherent in the structure of the
> person (Fromm 1973: 269-270).

To move beyond moral cruelty will require re-directing our attention, with
more of a focus on "freedom to" and less preoccupation with "freedom
from."

Is such a transition underway? Who could drive that re-direc-
tion of attention? On the one hand, it is clear that the mass machinery
for manufacturing consent continues to churn incessantly—especially
post 9/11. On the other hand, there exists a massive counterweight to the
morass of ameaning: parents who are attuned to their children and who
engage themselves meaningfully in the lives of their children; educators
who inspire passion and joy of learning and who encourage independent
thinking; organizations that value human beings and create a climate of
trust, commitment, and integrity both within the company and in relating
to those without; governmental officials who actually prize freedom of
speech and independent thought and who deplore the idea of blind conformity in the name of patriotism; and religious individuals and groups
who can distinguish the language of faith from the language of fact, and
who comprehend the nature of relatedness (my relationship to my father
and mother versus your relationship to your mother and father).

The future of moral cruelty hinges on attention; in a very significant way, we are what we attend to. To return to William James, a
person's "empirical thought depends on the things he has experienced,
but what these shall be is to a large extent determined by his habits of
attention" (James 1890/1950: 286). Our stream of consciousness, our
sense of meaning, our sense of self, and our moral reasoning—all must
be constructed from material to which we attend.

The question that we should ask ourselves as we ponder the future, then, is this: What in life is worthy of our attention?

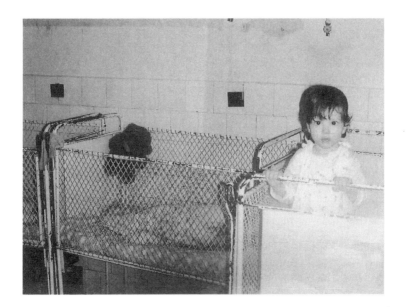

References

Ainsworth, M., M. Blehar, E. Waters, and T. Wall. 1978. *Patterns of attachment.* Hillsdale, NJ: Lawrence Erlbaum.

Alter, R. 1981. *The art of biblical narrative.* New York: Basic Books.

Ariarajah, S. W. 1985. *The Bible and people of other faiths.* Geneva: WCC Publications.

Ariés, P. 1962. *Centuries of childhood: A social history of family life.* New York: Knopf.

Arndt, J, J.L. Goldenberg, J. Greenberg, T. Pyszcynski, and S. Solomon. 2000. Death can be hazardous to your health: Adaptive and ironic consequences of defenses against the terror of death. In *Psychodynamic perspectives on sickness and health (*pp. 201-257). P.R. Duberstein and J.M. Masling, Eds. Washington, DC: American Psychological Association.

Aronson, E. 1999. *The social animal* (8th ed.). San Francisco: W.H. Freeman.

Bakunin, M. 1964. *The political philosophy of Bakunin.* G.P. Maximoff, Ed. New York: Free Press.

Barrington, L. W. 1997. Nation and nationalism: The misuse of key terms in political science. *Political Science and Politics*, 30, (4): 712-716.

Baumeister, R.F. 1999. *Evil: Inside human cruelty and violence*. New York: Freeman.

Becker, E. 1973. *The denial of death*. New York: Free Press.

Benn, S.I. 1967. Conscription and conscience. *Current Affairs Bulletin*, 40, (5): 67-80.

Bogosian, E. 1999. Spiritual thought for the day. *www.ericbogosian. com/letter23.html*.

Bowlby, J. 1969. *Attachment and loss. Vol. 1: Attachment*. New York: Basic Books.

Bowlby, J. 1973. *Attachment and loss. Vol. 2: Separation*. New York: Basic Books.

Brown, N. 1959. *Life against death: The psychoanalytic meaning of history*. Middletown, CT: Wesleyan University Press.

Brickman, P., D. Coates, and R. Janoff-Bulman. 1978. Lottery winners and accident victims: Is happiness relative? *Journal of Personality and Social Psychology*, 36: 917- 927.

Büber, M. 1970. *I and thou*. New York: Charles Scribner's Sons.

Campbell, J. 1988. *The power of myth*. New York: Doubleday.

Chomsky, N. 2002. *Understanding power: The indispensable Chomsky*. Peter Mitchell and John Schoeffel, Eds. New York: Free Press.

Cline, V., R.G. Croft, and S. Courrier. 1973. Desensitization of children to television violence. *Journal of Personality and Social Psychology*, 27, (3): 360-365.

Cohen, C., and V. Sherwood. 1991. *Becoming a constant object in psychotherapy with the borderline patient*. Northvale, NJ: Jason Aronson.

Csikszentmihalyi, M. 1997. *Finding flow: The psychology of engagement with everyday life*. New York: Harper Collins.

Csikszentmihalyi, M. 1999. If we are so rich, why aren't we happy? *American Psychologist*, 54, (10): 821-827.

Dasgupta, N., and A. Greenwald. 2001. On the malleability of automatic attitudes: Combating automatic prejudice with images of admired and disliked individuals. *Journal of Personality and Social Psychology*, 81, (5): 800-814.

Deaux, K., A. Reid, K. Mizrahi, and D. Cotting. 1999. Connecting the person to the social: The functions of social identification. In *The psychology of the social self. Applied social research* (pp. 91-113). Tom R. Tyler and Roderick M. Kramer, Eds. Mahwah, NJ: Lawrence Erlbaum.

DeMause, L. Ed. 1974. *The history of childhood.* New York: Psychohistory Press.

Devine, P.G. 1989. Stereotypes and prejudice: Their automatic and controlled components. *Journal of Personality and Social Psychology,* 56, (1): 5-18.

deWaal, F. 1996. *Good natured: The origins of right and wrong in humans and other animals.* Cambridge, MA: Harvard University Press.

Diener, E., J. Horwitz, and R.A. Emmons. 1985. Happiness of the very wealthy. *Social Indicators Research,* 16: 263-274.

DiMaggio, P. 1997. Culture and cognition. *Annual Review of Sociology,* 23, (1): 263-287.

Donald, M. 1991. *Origins of the modern mind: Three stages in the evolution of culture and cognition.* Cambridge, MA: Harvard University Press.

Drabman, R. S., M. H. Thomas, and G. J. Jarvie. 1977. Will our children care? New evidence concerning the effects of televised violence on our children. *Journal of Clinical Child Psychology,* 6, (1): 44-46.

Dunning, D. 2003. The zealous self-affirmer: How and why the self lurks so pervasively behind social judgement. *Motivated social perception: The Ontario symposium, Vol. 9. Ontario symposium on personality and social psychology* (pp. 45-72). Steven J. Spencer, Steven Fein, et al, Eds. Mahwah, NJ: Lawrence Erlbaum.

Edwards, R.C., M. Reich, and T.E. Weisskopf. 1986. *The capitalist system: A radical analysis of American society* (3rd ed.). Englewood Cliffs, NJ: Prentice Hall, Inc.

Erikson, E. 1963. *Childhood and society* (2nd ed.). New York: W.W. Norton.

Fein, S., E. Hoshino-Brown, P.G. Davies, and S. Spencer. 2003. Self-image maintenance goals and sociocultural norms in motivated social perception. *Motivated social perception: The Ontario symposium, Vol. 9. Ontario symposium on personality and social psychology* (pp. 21-44). Steven J. Spencer, Steven Fein, et al, Eds. Mahwah, NJ: Lawrence Erlbaum.

Festinger, L. 1957. *A theory of cognitive dissonance.* Oxford, England: Row, Peterson.

Frankl, G. 2001. *Foundations of morality: An investigation into the origin and purpose of moral concepts.* London: Open Gate.

Freud, S. 1901/1960. *The psychopathology of everyday life.* New York: W.W. Norton & Company.

Friedman, M. 1960. *Martin Büber: The life of dialogue.* Chicago: The University of Chicago Press.

Fromm, E. 1941. *Escape from freedom.* New York: Farrar & Reinhart, Inc.

Fromm, E. 1973. *The anatomy of human destructiveness.* New York: Holt, Rinehart and Winston.

Frost, C.J., and R. Bell-Metereau. 1998. *Simone Weil: On politics, religion and society.* London: Sage Publications, Ltd.

Gadamer, H. 1960/1989. *Truth and method.* New York: Crossroad/ Continuum.

Gadamer, H. 1987. *The relevance of the beautiful and other essays.* Nicholas Walker, Trans.; Robert Bernasconi, Ed. Cambridge; New York: Cambridge University Press.

Gatto, J. T. 2003. Against school: How public education cripples our kids, and why. *Harper's*, September ed.

Geertz, C. 1973. *The interpretation of cultures: Selected essays.* New York: Basic Books.

Gershoff E. 2002. Corporal punishment by parents and associated child behaviors and experiences: A meta-analytic and theoretical review. *Psychological Bulletin*, July; 128, (4): 539-579.

Glover, J. 2000. *Humanity: A moral history of the 20th century.* New Haven, CT: Yale University Press.

Goleman, D. 1995. *Emotional intelligence.* New York: Bantam Books.

Grolnick, W.S., E.L. Deci, and R.M. Ryan. 1997. Internalization within the family: A self-determination theory perspective. In *Parenting and children's internalization of values: A handbook of contemporary theory.* J. E. Grusec, and L. Kuczynski, Eds. New York: Wiley.

Hale, G.A., and M. Lewis. Eds. 1979. *Attention and cognitive development.* Princeton, NJ: Educational Testing Center.

Harton, H.C., and M.J. Bourgeois. 2004. Cultural elements emerge from dynamic social impact. In *The psychological foundations of culture.* M. Schaller, and C. Crandall, Eds. New York: Erlbaum.

Hawthorne, N. 1935. *The scarlet letter.* New York: The Heritage Press.

Hazan, C., and P. Shaver. 1990. Love and work: An attachment-theoretical perspective. *Journal of Personality and Social Psychology,* 59: 270-280.

Hegel, G. 1976. *Science of logic.* Atlantic Highlands, NJ: Humanities Press International.

Helfer, R., and H. Kempe. Eds. 1980. *The battered child* (3rd ed). Chicago: University of Chicago Press.

Helmuth, L. 2001. Cognitive neuroscience: Moral reasoning relies on emotion. *Science,* 293: 1971-1972.

Hong, Y., M.W. Morris, C. Chu, and V. Benet-Martinez. 2000. Multicultural minds: A dynamic constructivist approach to culture and cognition. *American Psychologist, 55, (7):* 709-720.

Huntington, S. 1993. The clash of civilizations? *Foreign Affairs,* Summer ed.

Inglehart, R. 1990. *Culture shift in advanced industrial society.* Princeton: Princeton University Press.

James, W. 1890/1950. *The principles of psychology.* New York: Dover Publications.

Jensen, D. 2000. *A language older than words.* New York: Context Books.

Kaplan, A. 1992. *Hatred, bigotry and prejudice: Definitions, causes and solutions.* Robert M. Baird and Stuart E. Rosenbaum, Eds. Amherst, NY: Prometheus Books.

Kaplan, G.A., E.R. Pamuk, J.W. Lynch, R.D. Cohen , and J.L. Balfour. 1996. Inequality in income and mortality in the United States: Analysis of mortality and potential pathways. *British Medical Journal,* 312: 999-1003.

Kimball, C. 2002. *When religion becomes evil.* San Francisco: Harper Collins.

Koch, S. 1965. The allures of ameaning in modern psychology. In *Science and human affairs.* R. Farson, Ed. Palo Alto, CA: Science and Behavior Books.

Koch, S. 1981. The nature and limits of psychological knowledge: Lessons of a century qua "science." *American Psychologist,* 36, (3*)*: 257-269.

Koch, S. 1999. *Psychology in human context: Essays in dissidence and reconstruction.* D. Finkelman and F. Kessel, Eds. Chicago: University of Chicago Press.

Kochanska, G., and R.A. Thompson. 1997. The emergence and development of conscience in toddlerhood and early childhood. In *Parenting and children's internalization of value: A handbook of contemporary theory* (pp. 53-77). J.E. Grusec, and L. Kuczynski, Eds. New York: Wiley.

Konner, M. 1983. *The tangled wing: Biological constraints on the human spirit.* New York: Harper & Row.

Kuczynski, L., and N. Hildebrandt. 1997. Models of conformity and resistance in socialization theory. In *Parenting and children's internalization of values: A handbook of contemporary theory.* J.E. Grusec, and L. Kuczynski, Eds. New York: Wiley.

Lau, I.Y., S. Lee, and C. Chiu. 2004. Language, cognition & reality: Constructing shared meanings through communication. In *The Psychological Foundations of Culture.* M. Schaller and C. Crandall, Eds. New York: Elrbaum.

Leary, D.E. 2001. One big idea, one ultimate concern: Sigmund Koch's critique of psychology and hope for the future. *American Psychologist,* 56, (5): 425-432.

Lifton, R. 2001. A conversation about surviving war, cults. *Austin American-Statesman*, September 23.

Loeb, P.R. 1999. *Soul of a citizen: Living with conviction in a cynical time*. New York: St. Martin's Griffin.

Lott, T. Ed. 2002. *Philosophers on race: Critical essays*. Malden, MA: Blackwell.

McKim, R., and J. McMahan, Eds. 1997. *The morality of nationalism*. New York: Oxford University Press.

Mencken, H.L. 1924. *The American mercury*. G.J. Nathan, Ed. New York: Knopf.

Merleau-Ponty, M. 1962. *Phenomenology of perception*. Atlantic Highlands, NJ: Humanities Press.

Mikulincer, M. 1997. Adult attachment style and the mental representation of the self. *Journal of Personality and Social Psychology,* 69: 1203-1215.

Mikulincer, M., and I. Orbach. 1995. Attachment styles and repressive defensiveness: The accessibility and architecture of affective memories. *Journal of Personality and Social Psychology,* 68: 917-925.

Miller, A. 1983. *For your own good: Hidden cruelty in child-rearing and the roots of violence*. Hildegarde and Hannum, Trans. New York: Farrar, Straus, & Giroux. [Originally published in German under the title *Am Anfang war Erziehung*].

Miller, W. 1949. American historians and the business elite. *The Journal of Economic History*, 9, (2): 184-208.

Morgan, G. 1997. *Images of organization,* (2nd ed.). Thousand Oaks, CA: Sage Publications.

Moustakas, C.E. 1972. *Loneliness and love*. Englewood Cliffs, NJ: Prentice-Hall.

Mouzelis, N. 1968. *Organisation and bureaucracy; An analysis of modern theories*. New York: Aldine de Gruyter.

Myers, D.G. 1993. *The pursuit of happiness*. New York: The Aquarian Press/ Harper Collins Publishers.

Norris, K. 2001. God was where God chose to be. In *From the ashes: A spiritual response to the attack on America* (pp. 50-54). Neale Donald Walsh, Ed. Emmaus, PA: Rodale.

Palmer, P. 1998. *The courage to teach.* San Francisco: Jossey-Bass.

Peel, J., and C.E. McCary. 1997. Visioning the "little red schoolhouse" for the 21st century. *Phi Delta Kappan*, 78, (9): 698-705.

Pettigrew, T.F., and R.W. Meertens. 1995. Subtle and blatant prejudice in western Europe. *European Journal of Social Psychology,* 25, (1): 57-75.

Pitts, L. 2003. Is Rudolph like Osama bin Laden? *Austin American-Statesman*, June 9.

Polanyi, M. 1958. *Personal knowledge; Towards a post-critical philosophy.* Chicago: University of Chicago Press.

Reich, W. 1941. Further problems of work democracy. B.G. Koopman and S.B. Heimbach, Trans. *Journal of Orgonomy*, 21, (2): 104-105.

Reingold, J. 1999. Special report: Executive pay: The numbers are staggering, but so is the performance of American business. So how closely are they linked? *Business Week Online*, April 1999 ed. http://www.businessweek.com/1999/99.

Ross, J.M. 1997. *The sadomasochism of everyday life: Why we hurt ourselves and others and how to stop.* New York: Simon & Schuster.

Sartre, J.P. 1956. *Being and nothingness: A phenomenological essay on ontology.* Hazel E. Barnes, Ed. New York: Washington Square Press, Pocket Books.

Schatzman, M. 1973. *Soul murder: Persecution in the family.* New York: Random House.

Sedikides, C. 1993. Assessment, enhancement, and verification determinants of the self-evaluation process. *Journal of Personality & Social Psychology*, 65, (2): 317-338.

Shaver, P., and C. Rubenstein. 1980. Childhood attachment experience and adult loneliness. In *Review of personality and social psychology*, 1: 42-73. L. Wheeler, Ed. Beverly Hills, CA: Sage Publications.

Smith, P.K., H. Cowie, and M. Blades. 1998. *Understanding children's development* (3rd ed.). New York: Blackwell.

Sobel, D. 1993. *Children's special places*. Tucson: Zephyr Press.

Solomon, J., and R. Solomon. 1993. *Up the university: Recreating higher education in America.* Reading, MA: Addison-Wesley.

Sroufe, L., and E. Waters. 1977. Attachment as an organizational construct. *Child Development,* 48: 53-64.

Steele, C.M. 1988. The psychology of self-affirmation: Sustaining the integrity of the self. In *Advances in experimental social psychology,* 21: 261-302. L. Berkowitz, Ed. New York: Academic Press.

Stern, D.N. 1985. *The interpersonal world of the infant: A view from psychoanalysis and developmental psychology.* New York: Basic Books.

Straus, M.A., and D.A. Donnelly. 1994-a. *Beating the devil out of them: Corporal punishment in American families.* New York: Lexington/Macmilllan.

Straus, M.A,. and D.A. Donnelly. 1994-b. Corporal punishment of adolescents by American parents. *Youth & Society,* 24, (4): 419-442.

Tajfel, H. 1982. Social psychology of intergroup relations. *Annual Review of Psychology,* 33: 1-39.

Thoma, S.J., J.R. Rest, and M.L. Davison. 1991. Describing and testing a moderator of the moral judgment and action relationship. *Journal of Personality and Social Psychology,* 61, (4): 659-669.

Thomas, M.H. 1982. Physiological arousal, exposure to a relatively lengthy aggressive film, and aggressive behavior. *Journal of Research in Personality,* 16, (1): 72-81.

Thomas, M.H., R.W. Horton, E.C. Lippicott, and R.S. Drabman. 1977. Desensitization to portrayals of real-life aggression as a function of television violence. *Journal of Personality & Social Psychology,* 35, (6): 450-458.

Tidwell, M-C., H. Reis, and P. Shaver. 1996. Attachment, attractiveness, and social interaction: A diary study. *Journal of Personality and Social Psychology,* 71, (4): 729-745.

Toffler, A. 1980. *The third wave.* New York: William Morrow and Company, Inc.

Vonnegut, K. 1966. *Mother night.* New York: Harper & Row.

Weil, S. 1957. *Intimations of Christianity among the ancient Greeks.* E.C. Geissbuhler, Trans. London: Routledge & Kegan Paul.

Weil, S. 1973. *Waiting for God.* New York: Harper & Row.

Wheatley, M. J. 1994. *Leadership and the new science: Learning about organization from an orderly universe.* San Francisco: Berrett-Koehler Publishers, Inc.

Wiesel, E. 1972. *Souls on fire; Portraits and legends of Hasidic masters.* Marion Wiesel, Trans. New York: Random House.

Wink, W. 1992. *Engaging the power: Discernment of resistance in a world of domination.* Minneapolis, MN: Fortress Press.

Index